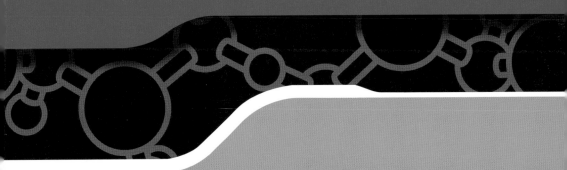

curriculum
connections

21st Century Science

Energy and Matter

BROWN
BEAR
BOOKS

Published by Brown Bear Books Limited

An imprint of:
The Brown Reference Group Ltd
68 Topstone Road
Redding
Connecticut 06896
USA
www.brownreference.com

Editorial Director: Lindsey Lowe
Managing Editor: Tim Harris
Project Director: Paul Humphrey
Editor: Andrew Solway
Designer: Barry Dwyer
Picture Researcher: Andrew Solway

**Library of Congress Cataloging-in-Publication
Data available upon request**

Picture Credits

Cover Image
Closeup image of soap bubble
(Shutterstock, Anyka)

CERN:
91

Jupiter Images:
26, 43 Photos.com; 55 PhotoObjects.net; 71
AbleStock.com

NASA:
7 NASA/STEREO/Naval Research Laboratory;
21 NASA/JPL-Caltech/L. Allen (Harvard-
Smithsonian CfA) & Gould's Belt Legacy
Team; 33; 39 NASA/MSFC/CXC/A. Bhardwaj
& R. Elsner et al. (X-ray); NASA/GSFC/L.
Perkins & G. Shirah (Earth model); 57
Dryden Flight Research Center; 67
NASA/Ensign John Gay, USS Constellation,
US Navy; 76 NASA/MSFC, E. Given; 85
NASA, ESA, CXC, JPL-Caltech, J. Hester and
A. Loll (Arizona State Univ.), R. Gehrz (Univ.
Minn.), and STScI; 89 NASA/QuikSCAT
Science Team, JPL; 99 NASA/HST/J. Morse/K.
Davidson; 105 NASA/CXC/M. Weiss

Shutterstock:
23; 50 Holger Mette; 64; 74 HP_photo; 81
Dean Pennala; 87 Oleg Nekhaev; 95 Ismael
Montero Verdu

Artwork © The Brown Reference Group Ltd

The Brown Reference Group Ltd has made
every effort to trace copyright holders of the
pictures used in this book. Anyone having
claims to ownership not identified above is
invited to contact The Brown Reference
Group Ltd.

Printed in the United States of America

Contents

Introduction

21st Century Science forms part of the Curriculum Connections project. Between them, the six volumes of this set cover all the key disciplines of the science curriculum: Chemistry, The Universe, Living Organisms, Genetics, The Earth, and Energy and Matter.

In-depth articles form the core of each volume, and focus on the scientific fundamentals. Each article relates to those preceding it, and the most basic are covered early in each volume. However, each article may be studied independently. So, for example, the Chemistry book begins with some relatively basic articles on atoms and molecules before progressing to more complex topics. However, the student who already has a reasonable background knowledge can turn straight to the article about carbon-hydrogen compounds to gain a more thorough understanding.

Within each article there are two key aids to learning that are to be found in color bars located in the margins of each page:

Curriculum Context sidebars indicate to the reader that a subject has particular relevance to certain key State and National Science and Technology Education Standards up to Grade 12.

Glossary sidebars define key words within the text.

A summary Glossary lists the key terms defined in the volume, and the Index lists people and major topics covered.

Fully captioned illustrations play a major role in the set, including photographs, artwork reconstructions, and explanatory diagrams.

About this Volume

We live in a material world. Everything is made of matter, and this matter changes when it is acted upon by various forms of energy: it moves, heats up, expands, glows, and interacts with other matter. The scientific discipline of classical physics—the main topic of this volume—is the study of matter: what it is, what its properties are, and how it relates to the forms of energy encountered in nature. These forms of energy include heat, light, electricity, magnetism, and sound.

The volume includes an introduction to the states of matter, together with some applications of the principles familiar in modern life. Another key theme of the book—energy and the forces through which it acts—is investigated, showing how matter can be acted upon in simple ways to make machines.

At the beginning of the 20th century, Albert Einstein and Max Planck set in train an even more fundamental discovery: that on a very small or a very large scale, matter and energy are themselves equivalent and interchangeable. These insights gave rise to a new era in physics, and required the development of the very different notions of quantum physics, which describes matter and energy on a very small scale. As scientists delved into the fundamental particles that make up atoms, they demonstrated the truth of the thesis that matter and energy are one.

While physicists have studied all these questions in theory, engineers and technologists have been quick to adopt them in all kinds of practical applications, from transport to microscopes, from information technology to the supply of energy resources. We are surrounded by machines, many of which we take for granted, which rely on quantum phenomena. This volume deals with the basic principles of physics and with their important modern applications.

Gases and Vapors

Everything in the world is made up of matter. All forms of matter are, in turn, made up of tiny particles called atoms, or of combinations of atoms called molecules. Much too small to be seen even with the most powerful optical microscopes, atoms and molecules account for the physical forms that matter may take, and for the way matter behaves in each of its various forms.

Curriculum Context

For all curricula, students should know that the states of matter (solid, liquid, gas) depend on molecular motion.

States of matter

All matter exists in one of three states: solid, liquid, or gas. Rocks are solids: they have a definite shape and obvious mass. The oceans are mainly a liquid—water. Like other liquids, water has no shape of its own and takes on the shape of its container. Air is a mixture of different gases, which make up a third kind of matter. A gas must be kept in a closed container or it escapes. Many substances can exist in more than one state. For instance, water is normally a liquid, but when it freezes it becomes solid ice.

Gases and vapors

Gas, or vapor, is the simplest form of matter. It has no structure, consisting of large numbers of independent particles (atoms or molecules). The individual particles have mass, which means that some gases are heavier than others. Because they are continually moving, the atoms or molecules possess kinetic energy—the energy of movement. The amount of kinetic energy depends on how fast they are moving, which in turn depends on the temperature of the gas: the hotter it is, the faster the molecules move around. Kinetic theory explains many phenomena connected with gases.

Air, the gas with which we are most familiar, has no container to hold it, and the force of gravity keeps it near the surface of the Earth. Gas pressure is a powerful natural force. The force or pressure of the

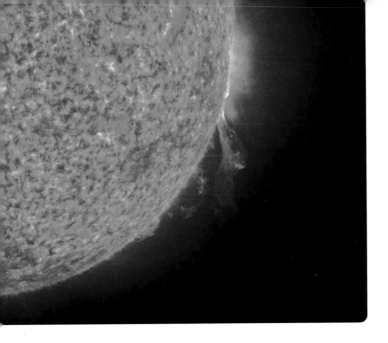

Magnetic forces at the Sun's surface create "hot spots," which shoot out huge arcs of plasma millions of miles (kilometers) into space. Plasma is a fourth state of matter, which exists on the Sun and other stars. In plasma, matter has so much energy that the atoms break up into charged fragments.

gases in the atmosphere derives from the weight of all the molecules above, which press on every square centimeter of every object in it. Atmospheric pressure is not constant: it falls with altitude. Weather results from occasional local variations in pressure and temperature. If the air molecules are heated the pressure falls and the hot air rises. Surrounding air masses rush in to replace the warm air, creating wind.

Most gases are studied in a container. The moving particles of a gas collide with one another and with the

Curriculum Context

For most curricula, students should understand how to apply the gas laws to relations between the pressure, temperature, and volume of any amount of an ideal gas or any mixture of ideal gases.

The Gas Laws

If extra pressure is applied to a gas its volume decreases, and the new volume is inversely proportional to the pressure (as long as the temperature does not change). This is known as Boyle's law (1662). But if the pressure of the gas is kept constant and it is heated, its volume increases, a relationship named Charles' law (1787). These laws can be stated mathematically.

If the volume of the gas is called V, its pressure p, and its absolute temperature (temperature above absolute zero) T, Boyle's law can be stated "$pV =$ constant", and Charles', "$V/T =$ constant". From these, a third gas law can be deduced: "$p/T =$ constant" (at constant volume, pressure is proportional to temperature). These laws explain why a balloon rises when the air inside is heated.

walls of the container. Particles striking the walls exert a force, and the effect of all these collisions accounts for the pressure that a gas exerts on its container.

Other gas phenomena

Kinetic theory explains other gas phenomena. Gas in a porous container loses particles gradually through the tiny holes in the material. Lighter gases have atoms or molecules with higher kinetic energy—they move faster and diffuse through the walls more quickly. The mid-19th century Scottish physicist Thomas Graham discovered that the rate at which a gas diffuses in this way is inversely proportional to the square root of its density. This principle has important applications. For example, in the nuclear industry, the two chief isotopes of the element uranium can be separated by letting a gaseous mixture of the two isotopes diffuse through a number of filters.

The English physicist John Dalton made another important discovery in 1801. If two or more gases are mixed, each exerts a pressure equal to the pressure it exerts on its own in the container. The particles of the individual gases collide but do not interfere with each other, and keep striking the walls of the container to exert pressure.

In 1811 the Italian physicist Amadeo Avogadro put forward the theory that, at the same temperature and pressure, equal volumes of all gases contain the same number of particles. The number of particles in a mole of a light element (0.07 ounces or 2 grams in the case of hydrogen) or of a heavier molecule such as carbon dioxide (1.55 ounces, 44 grams) is identical. The number—just over 600,000 billion billion—is called Avogadro's constant.

Isotopes

Forms of an element with the same numbers of protons in the nucleus but different numbers of neutrons.

Mole

The molecular mass of a substance expressed in grams.

Using Gas Pressure

The sails of ships and windmills were among the first human inventions to harness the power of gases under pressure—in this case, the pressure of gases in the atmosphere. Atmospheric pressure is also used in a simple lift pump for raising water from a well, acting on the surface of the water to lift it up. Other compressed gases, stored in metal cylinders or pumped from a container, can power equipment from pneumatic drills and jackhammers to aerosols such as perfume sprays.

Steam engines

Another use of gas under pressure sparked off the Industrial Revolution and was the key invention in the beginnings of modern technology. This was the steam engine. It was invented in the early 1700s and served as the major power source for industry and transport for more than 100 years, until it was replaced by electric motors and internal combustion engines. These newer sources of power themselves make use of gas pressure: turbines are used to drive the generators in power stations, while the pistons of an internal-combustion engine are powered by the expansion of the fuel gases after ignition.

The story of the steam engine began with Thomas Savery, an English engineer who in 1696 made a pump that employed a combination of steam and atmospheric pressure to pump water from mines. It relied on the fact that steam exerts a pressure but leaves a vacuum when condensed to form water. Sixteen years later Thomas Newcomen, from Cornwall in southwest Britain, built an engine that employed a cylinder and piston arrangement to transfer power to ordinary pumps. Then, beginning in 1769, James Watt designed steam engines that could drive industrial machinery more strongly and reliably than earlier water- or windmills. The new engines were also made

> **Curriculum Context**
>
> For many curricula, students should understand that steam engines and steam turbines are examples of practical heat engines. Steam at a high temperature T_H pushes on a piston or on a turbine and does work. Steam at a lower temperature T_L is then drawn off from the engine into the air.

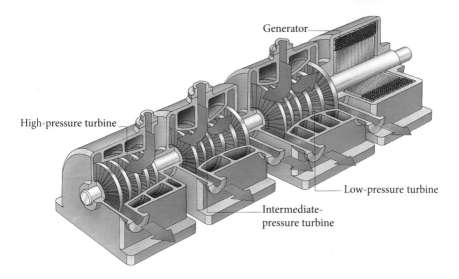

Generator

High-pressure turbine

Low-pressure turbine

Intermediate-
pressure turbine

In a steam turbine, the energy in high-pressure steam is extracted in three stages, of gradually reducing pressure. The turbine blades at each stage are designed to get the most energy from high, medium, or low pressure steam. All the blades are mounted on one shaft, which is connected to a generator.

into rail locomotives and traction engines for agriculture. These used the pressure of steam to drive a piston in a cylinder back and forth; the piston's motion was then transferred by linking rods to wheels. The application of steam power to ocean-going ships brought an additional transportation revolution, freeing sailors from the uncertainties of the winds and ocean currents.

Steam and gas turbines

Steam power is also the principal driving force for modern electric power stations. Steam is raised in a boiler, which heats water by burning coal, oil, or natural gas, or using heat from a nuclear reactor. Steam pressure spins the blades of turbines.

Gas turbines work on the same principle as a steam turbine, but the energy comes from the gases that result from burning a fuel such as kerosene. The jet engines used to power aircraft are gas turbines. They are also used in small scale and combined-cycle power stations. Air is compressed by the fans at the front of the engine and forced into the combustion chamber where ignition takes place. The exhaust gases are forced out of the rear in a powerful jet, creating a forward thrust. One advantage of the jet engine is that its performance improves with speed.

Combined-cycle power station

A power station in which exhaust gas from a gas turbine heats water to produce steam to power a steam turbine. The combination of gas and steam turbines allows a more efficient use of fuel.

The Liquid State

Oil and water are both liquids, but their physical properties are different. They can flow, yet their molecules are held together strongly enough by cohesive forces to take up a definite amount of space, though they have no shape. Both exert pressure, which for a liquid depends on its density and its depth. The liquid pressure occurring at the bottom of the sea is hundreds of times greater than at the surface.

At a particular point in a container of liquid, the pressure is the same in all directions. One special property of liquid is that, unlike a gas, it cannot be compressed. When pressure is applied at one point, it is immediately applied throughout the liquid: toothpaste, a thick liquid, squirts from the tube whether it is squeezed in the middle or at the end. This is an illustration of the principle of hydraulic mechanisms, which use the pressure caused by a relatively small force on a small piston to produce a very large force on a larger piston. Using a hydraulic jack, a person can single-handedly pump up enough pressure to lift a heavy truck.

Viscosity

Oil floats on water because oil is less dense. However, oil is thicker, or more viscous, than water, because of the greater attraction between its molecules. In a thick liquid such as oil or molasses, the molecules are strongly attracted to each other. They do not slide past each other easily, and the liquid is relatively difficult to pour.

Heating a viscous liquid decreases the molecular attraction; the liquid thins and becomes easier to pour. Increasing the pressure on a liquid forces the molecules closer together and increases viscosity. This is an important property of lubricating oils, which become

Curriculum Context

For most curricula, students should know that in solids the atoms are closely locked in position and can only vibrate; in liquids the atoms and molecules are more loosely connected and can collide with and move past one another.

more viscous with the high pressures between sliding parts and moving gears. If this were not so, the oil would be squeezed out and lubrication would fail, causing the parts to grind together.

Surface tension

Other physical properties of liquids may be explained by the cohesive force between molecules. The force between molecules at the surface, for example, creates the effect of a "skin" on the liquid. This is surface tension, which makes raindrops form spheres, holds soap bubbles together, and allows small insects to walk on water. Surface tension also makes it possible to float a small needle on water. Adding detergent to water with a needle floating on it causes the needle to sink, because detergent lowers surface tension. A liquid with low surface tension rises up a narrow capillary tube, which is why a porous material such as a sponge or tissue paper soaks up water. If a capillary tube is placed in a liquid that has a high surface tension, such as mercury, the level of the liquid in the tube falls.

Evaporation

At the surface of a liquid, some of the vibrating molecules escape from the surface. This is the process of evaporation, and it can be increased by raising the temperature of the liquid. At a sufficiently high temperature the liquid boils, and molecules rapidly leave the surface to form a gas or vapor.

Decreasing the pressure on a liquid reduces its boiling point. This is why water boils at a lower temperature at the top of a mountain (where atmospheric pressure is lower) than at sea level. Increasing the pressure on a liquid raises its boiling point, which is the principle of the pressure cooker.

Pressure cooker

A kitchen appliance used widely in the past to cook food more quickly. Today it has been largely superseded by the microwave.

The Solid State

Most solids exist in the form of crystals. Their shape reflects the regular arrangement of the atoms or ions within them, which are held together by strong interatomic forces, giving solids the properties of hardness, strength, rigidity, and high melting point. A weaker force holds together the molecules in amorphous solids such as glass, whose atoms do not form a regular pattern and more closely resemble those in a liquid.

Softer amorphous solids, such as waxes and many plastics, are composed of large molecules held together by weaker intermolecular forces. They lack strength and melt at low temperatures.

Even within the rigid lattice of a crystal, the individual atoms vibrate slightly. The amount of vibration depends on temperature. As a solid is heated, its atoms vibrate more vigorously, taking up more room; this is why most solids expand on heating. If a solid is made hot enough, the atomic vibrations overcome the interatomic forces and it melts to form a liquid. Ice melts at 32°F (0°C), sodium at 208°F (98°C), and caffeine at 460°F (238°C). A few solids, such as carbon, sublimate (turn directly into a gas) at a certain temperature, rather than melting.

Hardness

The hardness of a solid can also be explained in terms of its atomic structure. A good example is the element carbon, which occurs naturally in several forms, or allotropes. The crystalline form of carbon is diamond, in which each carbon atom is chemically bonded to four others in a tight lattice. Diamond is the hardest natural substance known, and it is extremely difficult to cut. It is used in industry in drilling and grinding even the hardest of metals. But in graphite, another allotrope of carbon, each atom is bonded to three others to form layers or sheets that are separated from each other by weaker molecular bonds. As a result, the sheets of atoms easily slide over each other, and graphite is so soft that it is commonly used as a lubricant.

On a scale of hardness devised in 1822 by the German mineralogist Friedrich Mohs, diamond is the hardest, assigned the number 10. The softest is the mineral talc (number 1). Hard metals—such as cast iron—tend to be brittle, and shatter easily. Soft metals, such as aluminum, copper, gold, and lead, can be drawn through dies to make wires, or beaten into thin sheets. Gold can be beaten into sheets so thin that strong light passes through them.

Elasticity

When a solid is stretched, its atoms are pulled slightly apart. The interatomic forces try to pull the atoms back to their original positions, and when the stretching force is removed, the solid snaps back to its original dimension. This is called elasticity. Hooke's law, formulated by the English physicist Robert Hooke, expresses the relationship between strain and stress on a solid.

A solid obeys Hooke's law up to a particular stretching force called the elastic limit. Stressed beyond this limit, the solid remains stretched slightly and does not return to its original dimensions. Stressed even further, it reaches its yield point, beyond which it continues to stretch with only a slight increase in the stretching force until eventually it breaks. Engineers use machines to stretch materials in this way and measure their tensile strength. Such measurements are essential in the design of aircraft, bridges, and ships.

Tensile strength

The ability of a material to resist longitudinal force (tension)—the force required to pull it apart.

Matter on the Move

An object that is moving along—such as a ball rolling along the ground—will go on moving forever unless something stops it. That "something" is a force; in the case of the ball it is friction with the ground, or a reactive force if the ball collides with another object. A force is also needed to start the ball rolling in the first place. The more massive an object is, the greater is the force needed to move it. It also takes a greater force to make an object accelerate quickly.

When a force causes an object to move, energy is used and work is done. The amount of work—measured in joules—is equal to the product of the force and the distance it moves. Energy can therefore be described as the capacity to do work; it also takes various forms. Mechanical energy may exist as one of two kinds of energy: kinetic energy or potential energy. An object, such as a rolling ball, has kinetic energy when it is moving. A weight that releases energy when it falls has potential energy due to its position. A compressed spring also stores potential energy.

Power is the rate of doing work. It takes a certain amount of power for somebody to carry a heavy box up a flight of stairs. But it takes much more power to run up the stairs carrying the same box. Power is measured in watts.

First law of motion

When a horse carrying a rider stops suddenly, the rider is thrown forward, often with painful consequences. This is an example of the first law of motion, stated by the English mathematician and philosopher Isaac Newton (1642–1727): an object remains at a state of rest or continues in uniform motion in a straight line, unless it is acted upon by external forces. The object's resistance to a change in its motion results from its

Curriculum Context

For many curricula, students should know that objects change their motion only when a net force is applied. Laws of motion are used to calculate precisely the effects of forces on the motion of objects.

mass or inertia; inertia throws the rider forward when the horse stops. A heavyweight rider is thrown harder because of greater momentum, which increases with mass and velocity (speed in a certain direction).

a

b

Centripetal force

Reaction

Action

c

Laws of Motion in Sport

(a) A football game provides many examples of Newton's first law of motion: force is needed to move an object or change its direction of movement. The force is the product of an object's mass and acceleration, so the heavier the player, and the faster he accelerates, the more force he brings to bear. (b) A hammer thrower spins around to build up the speed of the hammer. When the thrower lets go, the hammer flies off at a tangent to the circle. (c) The recoil felt by a rifleman as he shoots is a result of the conservation of momentum. The forward momentum of the bullet must be matched by the recoil of the rifle.

Second law of motion

Newton's first law of motion encapsulates the idea that any form of movement must involve at least one force. It states that the rate of a moving object's change of momentum is proportional to (and in the same direction as) the force producing the change. In most cases, the mass of the object does not change, and the law can be simplified to state simply that force equals the product of mass and acceleration:

$$F = ma.$$

Third law of motion

The third law of motion predicts what happens when two objects are involved. It states that if one object exerts a force on another, there is an equal and opposite force—called a reaction—that the second object exerts on the first. When the gases burn inside a rocket motor, they expand and push equally in all directions. The gases that exert a force on the closed front end of the combustion chamber cause a reaction—a force that pushes in the opposite direction and produces the thrust that propels the rocket.

Unlike a jet engine, a rocket is not propelled by exhaust gases pushing backward against the air; if this were so, a rocket would not be able to work in outer space, where there is no air at all. Because its design is based on the application of Newton's third law, a rocket may be technically described as a reaction motor.

Recoil

The recoil of a rifle illustrates a related principle which results directly from Newton's second and third laws of motion. According to the principle of conservation of momentum, the total momentum of two colliding objects after impact is equal to their total momentum before impact (as long as no external forces come into

Curriculum Context

For most curricula, students should know that the magnitude of any change in motion can be calculated using the relationship $F = ma$, which is independent of the nature of the force.

Curriculum Context

For most curricula, students should know that whenever one object exerts force on another, a force equal in magnitude and opposite in direction is exerted on the first object.

play). When a marksman fires a rifle, the forward momentum of the bullet (its mass multiplied by its velocity) equals the backward momentum of the weapon. The backward momentum is felt by the marksman as the recoil of the rifle. Because the rifle is considerably more massive than the bullet, it kicks back much more slowly than the bullet speeds forward. The heavier the rifle is, the harder the force of the kickback. The same effect may be observed even in a much smaller handgun, though with less kickback.

Circular motion

The key factor in any form of movement is velocity—speed in a given direction. If something moves at a uniform speed in a straight line, its velocity remains constant. But if something moves at uniform speed in a circle—such as a weight being swung around at the end of a piece of string—its velocity changes continuously because its direction of motion also keeps changing.

Newton's first law predicts that the rotating weight is subjected to a force that maintains its movement. This force, called centripetal force, acts inward toward the center of the circle, and at right angles to the direction of motion. Centripetal force can be felt as the tension in the string. If the string breaks, the force on the weight ceases to exist, and the weight flies off in the same direction in which it was traveling at the moment of release.

The Force of Gravity

Gravity is an important phenomenon that applies in physics, astronomy, space science, construction, and engineering. Gravity is a force of attraction that acts between any two objects, because of their masses.

Mass and weight

Mass is a measure of the quantity of matter. An object has the same mass on Earth, on the surface of the Moon, or in outer space, because it contains the same amount of matter wherever it is. But objects on Earth also have weight, which is the force of Earth's gravity acting on them. Weight is most properly measured in newtons, although for convenience it is often expressed in mass units such as kilograms or pounds.

Weight can be stated as mass multiplied by acceleration. For an object on Earth, therefore, weight is the object's mass multiplied by the acceleration due to gravity (also called the acceleration of free fall), a constant quantity in physics equal to nearly 26 feet per second per second (26 ft/sec^2, 9 m/sec^2). The acceleration due to gravity on the Moon, however, is only about 5.2 ft/s^2 (1.6 m/sec^2), which is why objects on the Moon weigh only about one-sixth as much as they do on Earth.

Force at a distance

Gravity is a force that can act at a distance. Indeed, the gravitational attraction of the Moon—although fairly weak—is strong enough over a distance of 238,750 miles (382,000 kilometers) to affect sea levels on Earth and cause the tides.

With increasing distance, gravity becomes weaker. The gravitational force of attraction between two objects is proportional to the product of their masses and inversely proportional to the square of the distance

Curriculum Context

For most curricula, students are expected to know that the force of gravity pulls objects toward the center of the Earth. This force of gravity is commonly called the weight of the object.

Measuring Gravity

The British physicist Henry Cavendish carried out a classic experiment in 1798 that provided the first measurement of the gravitational constant G and, derived from this, the mass of the Earth. Cavendish used an apparatus called a torsion balance, which measures the amount of twist in a wire, to measure the gravitational force of attraction between a pair of massive lead spheres and two much smaller, lighter spheres. The two light spheres were suspended from a wire, which twisted slightly as the lighter spheres were attracted to the heavier ones. The torsion balance measured the twisting force, or torsion.

between them. This relationship, called the universal law of gravitation, was worked out in about 1666 by the English scientist Isaac Newton (1642–1727).

The gravitational force between two objects acts between their centers of mass—the place at which all their mass appears to be concentrated. On Earth, the force of gravity acts between the center of the Earth and the center of the object.

Escape velocity and free fall

If a rocket wishes to escape totally from the Earth's gravity, it must reach a velocity known as the escape velocity. For Earth, the escape velocity equals 36.7 feet per second (11.2 km/sec).

A rocket or satellite that goes into orbit around the Earth does not need to reach escape velocity. It can orbit at any altitude as long as it is traveling fast enough to overcome Earth's gravity and remain in free fall. In free fall, the satellite's forward velocity is just great enough to keep it falling just beyond the curvature of the Earth.

Center of gravity

The center of mass of an object—also called its center of gravity—has an important influence on its stability.

The stability of an object can be defined by imagining a straight line drawn vertically down through its center of mass. With a pyramid standing on its base, a line drawn down from its center of mass passes through the base; the pyramid is said to be in stable equilibrium. If it is tipped slightly, its weight acts downward to pull it back into a stable position. But if the pyramid is balanced upside down on its point, the slightest movement makes it topple over; it is in unstable equilibrium.

A sphere or cylinder lying on its side is in neutral equilibrium—if it is displaced sideways, the center of mass still acts downward through the point of contact. Objects in stable or neutral equilibrium stay where they are unless acted on by an external force.

The Serpens South star cluster includes many protostars (very young, developing stars). Gravity is the force that makes large clouds of cosmic gas coalesce into large, dense gas balls. When they get large enough and hot enough, these gas balls turn into stars.

Mechanical Energy

An object that has mass and is moving possesses kinetic energy. It may be translational kinetic energy, for an object moving in a line, or rotational kinetic energy, for something spinning on its axis. An object with mass can also possess energy because of its position—called gravitational potential energy—or because it is deformed, like a stretched or compressed spring—called elastic potential energy. Kinetic and potential energy are the two types of mechanical energy.

Curriculum Context

Most curricula expect students to know how to calculate kinetic energy by using the formula $E = \frac{1}{2}mv^2$.

Kinetic and potential energy

The kinetic energy of an object is equal to the product of half its mass and the square of its velocity. Translational kinetic energy is proportional to the square of its velocity. This fact has important consequences. For example, if an object's velocity doubles, its kinetic energy increases four times. This is why the speed of a road vehicle—rather than its mass—is the chief factor that results in damage in a collision. A car traveling at 80 mph (135 km/h) has 16 times the kinetic energy of—and therefore a much greater impact than—a similar car that is traveling at a speed of only 20 mph (32 km/h).

An object with mass can also possess energy because of its position—called gravitational potential energy—or because it is deformed, like a stretched or compressed spring—called elastic potential energy. The value of gravitational potential energy possessed by or "stored" in an object is equal to the product of its mass, its height and the acceleration due to gravity (the acceleration of free fall). Thus, the heavier it is, or the higher it is, the greater is the potential energy.

Free fall

The ideal falling motion of an object subject only to the force of gravity. The acceleration of an object in free fall is approx. 9 m/sec^2.

Energy and work

All the various forms of mechanical energy can be made to do work. The translational kinetic energy of a rapidly moving pool cue, for example, transfers to the ball and makes it roll away; the rotational kinetic energy stored in a heavy flywheel can be made to operate machinery. Gravitational potential energy is not usually apparent until it is converted into kinetic energy. The gradually falling weights of an old-fashioned pendulum clock drive around the cog wheels, and the water stored behind a dam can be made to release its potential energy to turn the blades of a turbine. A simple example of stored elastic potential energy is a drawn bow, which releases its energy in an instant to fire an arrow to its target.

Oscillating energy

A swinging pendulum (see box overleaf) illustrates periodic, or oscillating, motion—motion that varies predictably with time. If the sideways displacement of a pendulum's weight is plotted against time, the resulting wave shape is known as a sine curve. A similar curve is obtained by plotting against time the displacement of a weight oscillating at the end of a

Curriculum Context

For many curricula, students should know how to calculate changes in gravitational potential energy near Earth using the formula (change in potential energy) $= mgh$, where h is the change in the elevation.

Snowboarding, skiing, and other downhill sports use the acceleration due to gravity to convert potential energy into kinetic energy.

Pendulums

In some systems potential and kinetic energy are continuously interchanged. One example is a pendulum, which consists of a weight swinging at the end of a rod or string. At the top of a swing, the weight has only potential energy. Then as it swings, gradually losing height, this energy is converted to kinetic energy. At the lowest point of the swing it has only kinetic energy and no potential energy. As the weight rises on the second half of the swing, potential energy is gradually restored. The rising weight does work against gravity. At the top of the swing the pendulum is momentarily stationary and has no kinetic energy. It is ready to swing down again.

vertical spring. Any motion that produces a sine curve in this way is called simple harmonic motion (SHM). The time for one complete oscillation is called the period of the motion, and the maximum displacement from the equilibrium position—sideways for the pendulum and up or down for the oscillating spring—is known as the amplitude.

There are many other examples of simple harmonic motion in physics, such as the rapid voltage oscillations of an alternating electric current or a radio wave.

Conservation of energy

Even in oscillating systems, the sum of the kinetic and potential energies always stays the same. This is one example of a wider—and important—principle in physics, called the conservation of energy. Formally, it states that the total amount of energy in any system remains constant, even though changes of energy from one form to another may take place.

Curriculum Context

For most curricula, students should know that the laws of conservation of energy and momentum provide a way to predict and describe the movement of objects.

Simple Machines

The Greek mathematician Archimedes (*ca.* 287–*ca.* 212 BCE) is credited with saying that, given a lever long enough, he could move the world. The lever is one of the simplest of early machines. Using a long pole pivoted over a flat stone, a person can lift and move a massive object such as a boulder.

There are two basic types of simple machines: the lever and the inclined plane. These mechanical devices multiply the limited force available to humans and animals to help them make things move.

The same mechanical principles that apply to simple machines like levers and pulleys are still behind the designs of the most complicated modern machines, from gearboxes to escalators and giant cranes.

Levers

The simplest kind of lever, described above, has the pivot situated between the point at which the effort is applied and the point at which the load is raised. It is called a class one lever. Another example is a seesaw, on which a small child sitting at one end can lift a large adult sitting nearer the pivot on the other side.

This example illustrates the key reason for using levers: if the pivot is closer to the load than the effort, a small effort can produce a large effect. A long lever that uses a small effort to lift a heavy load has a large force ratio or mechanical advantage, defined as the load (the output force) divided by the effort (the input force). Class one levers also combine in pairs to form scissors and shears.

There are two other types of levers. A class two lever has the effort and the load on the same side of the pivot (known technically as a fulcrum), as in a wheel-

Curriculum Context

For most curricula, students should know how levers confer mechanical advantage and how this principle can be applied to many common devices.

barrow. In a class three lever, the effort is between the load and the fulcrum, as in a pair of tweezers or the muscles that bend a human arm.

For a long lever, the effort has to move a long way to produce only a small movement of the load. It is described as having a small distance ratio (or velocity ratio)—the distance moved by the load divided by the distance moved by the effort. The efficiency of any machine is the usable energy output divided by the energy input. For a lever, it is the same as the force ratio divided by the distance ratio. Overall, the class one lever is an efficient machine.

Pulleys and gears
The wheel and axle is an extension of the lever principle. It is employed in a windlass, gear wheels, belt drives and pulleys. Pulleys and gears provide a mechanical advantage, allowing a small effort to move a large load.

Cranes have powerful motors that allow them to lift loads many times heavier than a human can manage. However, for heavy loads they also use a pulley system to increase their mechanical advantage.

A single pulley merely changes the direction of the effort and, because of the friction in the pulley, may actually need an effort that is larger than the load. But for two pulleys (neglecting friction), the force ratio is 2—a given weight can lift a load weighing twice as much. For four pulleys the force ratio is 4, and so on: the mechanical advantage equals the number of pulleys.

Distance ratios get smaller as the number of pulleys increases, because the effort has to move longer distances to raise the load. The theoretical efficiency remains the same (at 100 percent), but in practice friction takes a greater and greater toll, so that multiple pulleys are much less efficient than single ones. But if a pulley block is the only machine available—as it was for centuries—providing more force to overcome friction still enables muscle power to be multiplied and to achieve results impossible for the unaided human.

Inclined planes

An inclined plane hardly seems to be a machine at all. At its most basic, it is a slope up which a load must be pushed. But it is much easier to push the load up the slope than to lift it vertically to the same overall height. There is a mechanical advantage, equal to the length of the slope divided by the height—the gentler the slope, the greater the mechanical advantage.

Two applications of the inclined plane are the wedge and the screw. A wedge may be driven under a load to lift it, or into something to split it. If an inclined plane is wrapped around a cylinder, a helical inclined plane results: a screw. Turning the screw forces it into a material, like a spiral wedge. As well as screws and nuts, the screw is the basis of devices such as the the screw jack and the worm gear.

Worm gear

A rod with a screw thread (the worm) that meshes with a toothed wheel (the worm wheel). It is used to convert rotary motion in one shaft to rotary motion in another shaft at right angles to the first. It can also change the speed and power of the rotation.

Heat Energy

When an object gets hot, the heat energy is stored in its atoms, which continuously vibrate—the more they vibrate, the hotter the object becomes. Heat is a form of kinetic energy, the energy of motion of the vibrating atoms.

Heat is regarded as a separate type of energy, capable of being converted into all other forms. If anything is made hot enough it gives off light, and in a thermocouple—a type of electrical circuit—heat is converted directly into electricity. Other forms of energy can also be turned into heat: electricity flowing in a high-resistance wire, and friction between two moving surfaces in contact, both generate heat.

Transferring heat

Heat can travel from place to place. In a bar of metal heated at one end, for example, the vibration of the hot atoms is passed on to their neighbors so that heat gradually travels along the bar toward the unheated end. This type of heat transfer is called conduction, and materials such as metals are good conductors of heat.

Heat can also be transferred in the motion of a hot gas or liquid. A warm gas is less dense than a cold one and so it tends to rise, causing air currents in a heated room, or large movements of air which result in changes in patterns of weather. This type of heat transport is called convection, and the resulting movements of gas or liquid are convection currents.

Heat can also move by radiation—the heat from the Sun reaches the Earth through the vacuum of space by this method. Any object whose temperature is above absolute zero emits heat radiation, although the rates of emission become significant only at high temperatures.

Insulation

Another way of defining heat is to regard it as energy in transit from one object to another because they have different temperatures. A knowledge of how heat travels can be useful in stopping unwanted heat flow. One way of keeping something warm is to surround it by a poor conductor—a thermal insulator such as plastic foam—to prevent heat from being conducted away. In a similar way, quilted or padded clothing helps keep people warm in cold climates. A vacuum flask also prevents the other kinds of heat transfer, keeping cold liquids cold or hot liquids hot.

Measuring heat

Heat is measured in joules. But some applications use different, and older, heat units. For example, dieticians express the energy content of food in kilocalories (sometimes expressed as Calories, with a capital C). The calorific value of a food is the amount of energy released when it is completely burned. Sugar has 39 calories per gram; fats (such as butter) have 76 calories per gram.

Kilocalorie

1 kilocalorie = the amount of heat needed to raise the temperature of a kilogram of water through 1 degree Celsius.

Cold

Hot

Heat conduction

Warm

A metal bar heated at one end illustrates the kinetic theory of heat—that is, the atoms in any object at a temperature above absolute zero are in a state of constant vibration. The hotter they get, the more they vibrate; and the vibrations are passed on to neighboring atoms. This last effect accounts for the conduction of heat along solid objects.

Thermodynamics

Thermodynamics studies the ways in which heat is transferred between objects and the ways in which other forms of energy may be converted into heat—and vice versa. Thermodynamics is a branch of physics, but engineers also apply it in designing heat engines, and chemists use it to gain a better understanding of chemical reactions (which all involve an exchange of heat).

History

In 1849 the British physicist James Joule carried out experiments to determine the exact relationship between mechanical energy and heat. He worked out the mechanical equivalent of heat as about 4.2 joules of work for each calorie of heat produced.

First law of thermodynamics

A year later the German scientist Rudolf Clausius summed up Joule's results as follows: in any process, energy can be changed from one form into another but it can never be destroyed or created. This became known as the first law of thermodynamics. It has also been described as the law of conservation of energy.

Every heat engine has a high-temperature reservoir—in an internal combustion engine it is the exploding mixture of air and fuel in the cylinders. As it performs work (mechanical output), some heat passes to a low-temperature reservoir—in an internal combustion engine the exhaust gases.

Second law of thermodynamics

The second law of thermodynamics can be put in everyday terms as "heat will not flow uphill" or, more formally, heat will only flow of its own accord from a hotter object to a colder one. Stand a cup of hot coffee on a cold platter, and heat will pass from the cup to the platter until they are both at the same

A refrigerator can be thought of as a heat engine working backward. Outside work is done to make it take in heat from a low-temperature reservoir (inside the fridge) and pass it to a high-temperature reservoir (its surroundings).

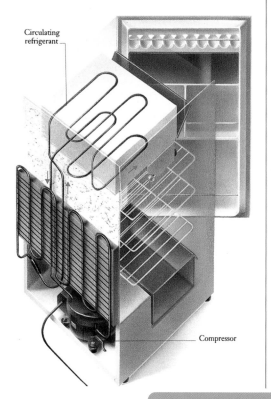

Circulating refrigerant

Compressor

temperature. One result of the second law is that no heat engine can ever be totally efficient. It cannot convert all the heat provided to it into mechanical energy unless the low-temperatrure reservoir (its surroundings) are at a temperature of absolute zero.

Entropy and the third law

The second law can also be stated in terms of another physical quantity called entropy. For a system possessing energy, entropy is a measure of the disorder of a system. For any irreversible process, the total entropy of a system (and its surroundings) always gets larger. As entropy increases, less energy is available for doing work. The link between energy and entropy gives rise to some interesting theories. One of these says that eventually all the energy in the Universe will become distributed evenly.

Like heat energy, entropy decreases with falling temperature. This fact gives rise to the third law of thermodynamics, which states that, at absolute zero, the entropy of a substance is zero.

There is another law of thermodynamics, called the zeroth law. In its simplest form it says that no heat will flow between two objects at the same temperature.

Curriculum Context

For most curricula, students should know that entropy is a quantity that measures the order or disorder of a system and that this quantity is larger for a more disordered system.

Absolute zero

The lowest possible temperature (0 K, −459°F or −273°C), at which atoms and molecules have zero energy.

Heating and Cooling

The specific heat capacity of a substance is the amount of heat needed to raise one kilogram of the substance through 1 degree Kelvin. Materials differ in their heat capacity. Water, for example, has a specific heat of more than $4 \text{ J g}^{-1} \text{ K}^{-1}$, while that of gold is less than 0.2.

Latent heat

When a pure solid is heated, its temperature rises in a regular way until, when it reaches a certain temperature, it continues to absorb heat without its temperature rising further; the substance then melts. Once it is completely liquid, its temperature starts rising again.

The extra heat needed to make the change of state happen is called the latent heat of fusion. The same amount of heat is released when a liquid is cooled until it freezes. More latent heat—the latent heat of vaporization—is also required to make a liquid at its boiling point change into a gas or vapor. These latent heats weaken the attractive forces between atoms or molecules, turning a solid into a liquid or a liquid into a gas. When a substance cools and turns from gas to liquid, or liquid to solid, the latent heats are emitted.

The Joule–Kelvin effect

As a hot object cools, it transfers heat to its surroundings. To make it colder than the surroundings, heat has to be removed from it. When a gas flows through a small hole into a larger container, its temperature drops as its pressure falls (because heat is used up in pushing the gas molecules farther apart). Called the Joule–Kelvin, or Joule–Thompson, effect, this is the principle of a refrigerator, in which the heat absorbed by an expanding gas is taken from the surrounding interior of the refrigerator. The effect also explains why an aerosol spray feels so cold as it emerges from its container, though the exterior of the container does not feel cold itself.

Cryogenics

The Joule–Kelvin effect can be used to liquefy a gas and create very low temperatures. Usually the gas, such as air, is first compressed and cooled to about –25°C in a refrigerator, and then cooled even further to –160°C by making it do work by expansion in a turbine. Finally the cold air expands through a narrow aperture and turns to a liquid (at about –180°C). Other gases liquefy at much lower temperatures, such as hydrogen (–259°C) and helium (–271°C).

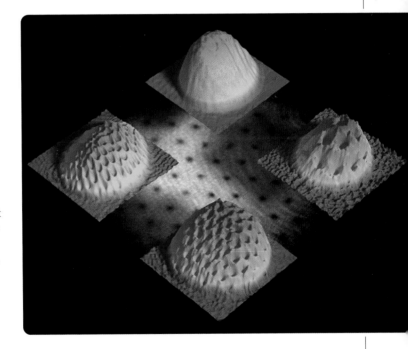

This computer model shows the whirlpools in a Bose–Einstein condensate made from sodium gas. In 1995, two groups of US scientists managed to make Bose–Einstein condensates for the first time. They received the 2001 Nobel Physics Prize for their research.

Cryogenics encompasses the techniques for producing such cold environments. The usual way of rapidly cooling substances under study is to immerse them in a bath of liquid gas, which can reach temperatures as low as 3 K (–454°F, –270°C). Researchers in laboratories have achieved temperatures that come within a hundred billionth (10^{-11}) of a degree of absolute zero (0 K). Absolute zero itself is a purely theoretical temperature that is actually impossible to achieve.

Low-temperature properties

Materials can have very strange properties at such low temperatures. At a low enough temperature, liquid helium, for instance, loses all its viscosity and becomes a superfluid. It climbs up the walls of its container, leaving it empty. At a few billionths of a degree above absolute zero, atoms cease to have individual identity, and fuse to form a Bose–Einstein condensate. This was first observed in 1995.

Ceramic

A strong, brittle, non-metallic material made by heating the raw materials to high temperatures.

At very low temperatures some metals and ceramics lose all their electrical resistance and become superconductors. If an electric current is made to flow in a circuit of superconductors, it goes on flowing forever without the need for an external source of voltage. Superconducting magnets are used in devices such as nuclear magnetic resonance machines and maglev (magnetic levitation) trains.

"High-temperature" superconducting materials can operate at temperatures above –321 °F (–196 °C)—the temperature of liquid nitrogen. Such superconductors are relatively simple to keep cool. This has opened the way for some industrial applications. However, the search continues for high-temperature superconductors that are relatively simple and cheap to manufacture.

Measuring and Using Heat

Temperature is the degree of hotness of an object. It can be measured in terms of any of several physical properties that change with temperature. An ordinary thermometer makes use of the expansion of a liquid in a narrow glass tube. The expansion of the liquid—usually dyed alcohol or mercury—is shown on a scale calibrated in degrees. The positions of the calibrations are determined by two so-called fixed points, which for an ordinary thermometer are usually the freezing and boiling points of water.

Temperature scales

On the Celsius (formerly centigrade) scale, the freezing and boiling points of water are 100 degrees apart. On the Fahrenheit scale they are 180 degrees apart: the freezing point of water is 32°F, the boiling point 212°F.

Physicists and other scientists often use the absolute, or Kelvin, temperature scale, which runs from absolute zero (0 K) and has degrees that are the same size as Celsius degrees. On this scale, the freezing point of water is just over 273 K and its boiling point is 373 K.

Other ways of measuring temperature

The electrical resistance of a metal—its ability to carry an electric current—also varies with temperature. This phenomenon is used in a platinum resistance thermometer, which measures temperature by the resistance of a piece of platinum wire.

Very high temperatures can be measured by making use of the fact that the speed of sound through a gas depends on its temperature. A microphone on one side of the furnace picks up a series of clicks generated by an electric spark on the other side. A computer measures the temperature by calculating the time taken by the sounds to reach the microphone.

Curriculum Context

For many curricula, students should understand that when a thermometer is inserted into a substance and the temperature is measured, the average atomic or molecular energy of motion is being measured.

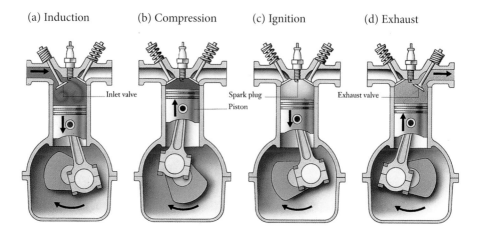

(a) Induction (b) Compression (c) Ignition (d) Exhaust

Inlet valve
Spark plug
Piston
Exhaust valve

Probably the most important type of heat engine is the internal combustion engine. The most common kind of engine uses the four-stroke Otto cycle. The key stages are: (a) induction—the fuel/air mixture enters the cylinder; (b) compression—the piston moves up; (c) ignition—the spark plug explodes the fuel and the piston moves down; and (d) exhaust—the spent gases leave the cylinder.

Heat engines

To put heat to good use, it is often changed into another form of energy. The function of a heat engine—such as an internal combustion engine, gas or steam turbine, or rocket—is to convert heat into mechanical energy. In each of these, heat makes gases that are the products of combustion expand and move a piston or turbine, or create thrust. The efficiency of such engines depends mainly on the difference in temperature (and therefore the energy content) between the gases before and after they have done their work. This way of studying engines was first suggested by the French engineer Nicolas Sadi Carnot (1796–1832).

Heat engines work on a cycle of changes involving the intake, combustion, expansion, and exhaust of hot gases. But even a theoretically perfect engine is less than 100 percent efficient. In real engines, efficiency—the ratio of heat input to heat output—is usually between 40 and 50 percent because of energy losses such as friction, waste heat and sound.

Magnets and fields

As early as the second century BCE, magnets were used by Chinese navigators. These ancient sailors found that if they suspended a piece of the mineral lodestone on a thread, it always lined up in a north–south direction and could be used as a primitive compass.

The ancient Greeks discovered that a piece of amber rubbed with fur attracted pieces of straw and other scraps, in much the same way that a magnet attracts small pieces of metal. However, in this case the origin of the attraction is not magnetism but static electricity. The Greek word for amber is elektron, which is the root of the words electron and electricity. Electricity and magnetism are produced by the behavior of electrons and other particles in atoms.

Causes of magnetism

A magnet is piece of iron or other metal that attracts or repels a similar nearby piece of metal. The effect can be traced to the subatomic particles that make up the atoms of the metal.

As electrons (which are negatively charged) orbit the nuclei of the atoms, they spin and generate a small magnetic field. The tiny atomic magnets line up with each other to form magnetic regions called domains. In a piece of iron or steel, there are millions of domains, some pointing one way, some another, so that there is no overall magnetic field. But if the metal is placed in an external magnetic field, the domains line up parallel with the field and to each other. Their individual tiny fields combine to form a single large one, and the metal becomes a magnet.

Magnetic field
The region around a magnet in which its magnetic forces act.

Magnetic properties of materials

The magnetic properties of a material depend on the number of electrons and how they spin. Ferromagnetic materials—such as iron, cobalt, or nickel—are ones in which, within the atoms in the domains, the spins of the electrons line up in the presence of an external magnetic field. Below a certain temperature the magnetization persists even when the external field is removed, and the material becomes a permanent magnet. Other ferromagnetic materials include ferrites—ceramic substances that are a combination of cobalt, zinc, or nickel with an iron oxide. Ferrites can be used to make extremely powerful permanent magnets.

Paramagnetic substances acquire magnetic properties in the direction of an external magnetizing field because their component "atomic magnets" line up. But the magnetization disappears when the external field is removed. In a few substances—which are diamagnetic—the temporary magnetization is in the opposite direction to the external field.

Magnetic fields

In a bar-shaped magnet, the magnetic field appears to originate at a point near one end of the bar and extend into space, curving around to a point near the other end. The two ends are called the poles of the magnet— north and south—and the field can be represented as lines of force joining them. Magnetic poles always occur in north–south pairs. A line of force can be thought of as the path a single pole would take as it moved in response to the magnetic forces acting on it.

North and south poles

Another property of magnetic poles is that similar ones—such as two north poles—repel each other, and dissimilar ones attract each other. Their magnetic fields either join together or push each other apart. In fact, any two magnetic poles exert a force on each other which is proportional to the product of their strength divided by the square of the distance between them. For this reason, a magnetic field falls off fairly rapidly with distance from the magnet.

The needle in a compass is a small pivoted magnet. Its north-seeking end (actually a north pole) always points in the direction we call north. For this to happen, there must be a south magnetic pole near the Earth's North Pole. It is as if the Earth has a huge bar magnet along its axis, making compass needles all over the world align with the Earth's magnetic field and point north and south. Electric currents in the molten iron core of the Earth give rise to this magnetic field. The magnetic poles do not coincide exactly with the geographic poles, however, and they move slowly from year to year. Navigators must take account of this when using a compass.

The Earth's magnetic field extends into space for thousands of miles (kilometers) as the magnetosphere. The shape of the magnetic field is distorted by the effects of the solar wind.

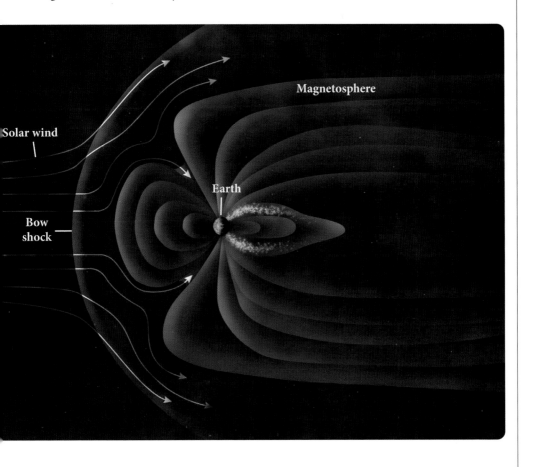

Static Electricity

When a nonmetallic object, such as a plastic comb, is rubbed on a piece of dry cloth or fur, it is able to attract light objects such as hair, like a magnet picking up paper clips. This phenomenon is caused by changes in the atoms in its surface. Friction "rubs off" some of the electrons on the atoms of the comb. Because electrons carry a negative charge, the comb is left with a positive charge. Static electricity is the accumulation of these electrostatic charges.

Two combs charged up in this way repel each other. But when a charged comb is brought near scraps of paper, its positive charge causes electrons to accumulate on the closest part of each piece of paper, giving them a negative charge. This transfer of charge is called electrostatic induction. The negatively-charged paper is then attracted to the positively-charged comb.

Charges and fields

A key fact of electric charges is that dissimilar charges attract each other and similar charges repel. A charged object influences the region surrounding it: in other words, a charge creates an electric field.

Insulator

A nonmetallic element or compound that resists the flow of electricity through it.

When an insulator is placed in an electric field, the field exerts a force on the electrons in it. If the field is strong enough, the electrons are torn from their atoms and flow through the material, carrying charge. This is what happens in lightning. The huge electric field between charged clouds, or between clouds and the ground, breaks down the insulating properties of the air, and a giant spark jumps across. There is an accompanying flash of light and a shock wave in the air.

If one object has more charge than another, it is said to have a higher electric potential. When two charged objects are connected, positive charges flow from the one of higher potential to the one with lower potential

Large potential differences are produced by electrostatic machines such as the Van der Graaff generator. It can produce potentials of up to 6 million volts—equivalent to a bolt of lightning—for particle accelerators and other research apparatus. Charges from a high-voltage supply are carried by a conveyor belt and stored on a semicircular metal dome.

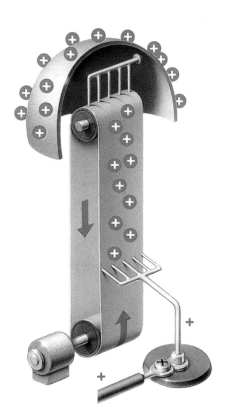

until their potentials are the same. The greater the initial potential difference between the two, the more readily charge flows between them. Another term for potential difference is voltage, and such differences are measured in volts. The amount of charge on an object is measured in coulombs. Charge flow involves changes in energy, and therefore is work.

Charges on atoms

Groups of atoms, single atoms, and even subatomic particles can carry electric charges. Any molecule (group of atoms) or single atom carrying a charge is called an ion. The metals sodium, calcium, and iron, for example, form positive ions whereas chlorine and bromine form negative ones. Ions are the current carriers in discharge tubes and fluorescent tubes.

The chief subatomic particles are the electron (with a single negative charge) and the proton (with a positive charge). Because protons are concentrated in the nucleus of the atom, the nucleus itself has an overall positive charge, which, in a non-ionized atom, is balanced by an equal negative charge contributed by the electrons orbiting the nucleus.

Ions and subatomic particles attract and repel each other following the rules of static electricity; unlike charges attract each other, and like charges repel.

Electric Current

An electric current, measured in amperes (amps), consists of a flow of electrons. For a nonmetallic substance such as plastic or glass, it takes a huge potential difference across the material to make the atoms' electrons break away and carry charge. But with metals, even a small potential difference—usually known as a voltage—causes a current to flow. Most metals are good conductors of electricity.

Current flow

Before 20th-century scientists discovered the key role played by electrons in electricity, they had to assign a direction to current flow, and they established the convention that it flows from a point of positive charge to one of negative charge. In fact, the negatively-charged electrons flow the other way around a circuit, from negative to positive, but the convention about the direction of an electric current has been retained. An atom or molecule that has lost an electron (or electrons) is left with a positive charge and is called an ion. Ions, too, can be conductors of electric current.

Not all metals conduct electricity equally well, depending on their availability of electrons. The best conductors include aluminum, copper, gold, and silver. Because they are less expensive than gold and silver, copper and aluminum are the ones commonly used to make wires and cables for carrying electric current.

Curriculum Context

Most curricula expect students to be able to solve problems involving Ohm's law. Ohm's law gives the relationship between the current *I* that results when a voltage *V* is applied across a wire with resistance *R*.

Ohm's Law

The property of a substance that opposes the flow of electricity is known as resistance. It can be measured by applying a voltage and measuring the current flow. The German physicist Georg Ohm (1787–1854) established the relationship between voltage, current, and resistance. Ohm's law states that, for a given material, resistance (R) equals voltage (V) divided by

Electricity is one of the most useful and versatile forms of energy. Electric lighting was one of the earliest applications and is today probably the most important use of electric current. Many machines rely on electric motors, and the vast range of electronic devices depend on electricity.

current (I): $R = V/I$. The unit of resistance is the ohm, and ohms therefore equal volts divided by amps.

Energy conversion

Electricity, because of its ability to move charges, is a form of energy. It can therefore be converted into other forms of energy. For example, when an electric current flows along a piece of wire, the wire is heated. The higher the resistance of the wire, the hotter it gets. If it gets hot enough, it becomes incandescent and gives off light. Electric heaters and electric lamps both use coils of wire to produce heat or light in this way.

Incandescent

The emission of light by a hot body. The color of light emitted is related to the body's temperature.

Magnetic field

Another result of the flow of a current along a wire is the production of a magnetic field. The lines of force of the field take the form of concentric circles around the wire. If the wire is wound into a coil, the magnetic fields combine to give lines of force that resemble those of a bar magnet. The strength of the resulting magnet—called an electromagnet—can be increased by putting a length of magnetic material such as iron along the axis of the coil.

Producing Electric Current

Any device that makes electrons flow along a wire is a current generator. There are many kinds of generator. Some are chemical, but the most important kind is mechanical and depends on the interaction of electricity and magnetism.

Mechanical generators

When a length of wire moves in a magnetic field, a current is induced in the wire. If the wire is bent into a coil (or series of coils) and turned in the field between the poles of a magnet, a simple rotating switch can make it produce a continuous flow of electricity. The device for converting mechanical energy into electrical energy—the dynamo—was first conceived more than 150 years ago by the English scientist Michael Faraday (1791–1867).

Cells and batteries

Thirty years before Faraday's discovery, an Italian physicist, Alessandro Volta (1745–1827), found another way of making electric current. He created a voltaic pile, what we would now call a battery, or cell.

In a simple Daniell cell, a piece of copper (called an electrode) dips into a solution of copper sulfate (the electrolyte), separated by a porous barrier from the other electrode—a piece of zinc dipping into dilute sulfuric acid. At the zinc electrode, zinc dissolves in the acid to form zinc ions, releasing electrons. These move as an electric current along a wire connecting the electrodes. Ions travel in solution between the electrodes, completing the circuit.

Electrons arriving at the copper electrode combine with positive copper ions from the electrolyte to form metallic copper. The zinc electrode has a negative charge and is called the cathode, while the copper electrode is the positive pole, or anode.

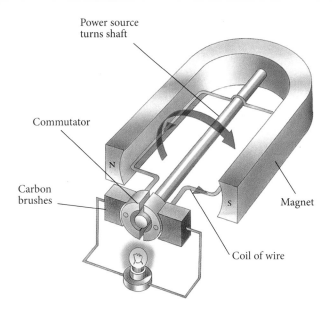

Power source turns shaft

Commutator

Carbon brushes

N

S

Magnet

Coil of wire

The principle of the dynamo is best explained by a single coil attached to a shaft rotating in a magnetic field. The commutator keeps current flowing in the same direction.

The Daniell cell is an example of a primary cell. When the cell's chemicals are used up, it ceases to function. Dry batteries, as used in flashlights and personal stereos, are also primary cells. Secondary cells, such as the large battery (or accumulator) that starts a car engine, can be recharged and used again and again. An external voltage applied across the electrodes reverses the current-generating reactions and restores the cell to working order.

Direct and alternating current

The electricity generated by dynamos and batteries is called direct current (DC), because it flows in one direction. That is the purpose of the switching device in a dynamo, but in a machine without one—called an alternator—the current flows first in one direction and then in the other. This kind of electricity, called alternating current (AC), is supplied by the mains to houses and industry. Alternating current is preferred because, for a given voltage, it can be carried along thinner wires and can easily be converted to another voltage using a transformer. The circuits in electronic equipment, such as televisions and hi-fi systems, use direct current. If they are connected to an AC supply, the current is first converted to DC by a rectifier.

Transformer

A device in which alternating current of one voltage can be raised or lowered to another voltage.

Generating Electricity

Electricity is an extremely useful form of energy because it can conveniently be distributed to wherever it is required, and once there, it is easy to convert into other forms of energy—that is, to do work. The commercial generation of electricity is a major industry. It has to make use of other forms of energy, which are converted into mechanical energy to drive electric generators.

Energy sources

Often the prime energy is heat from a fossil fuel such as coal, oil, or natural gas, which is burned to generate steam for driving turbines (which turn the generators). Alternatively, heat from a nuclear reactor can be used to make steam for steam turbines. Flowing water, often coming from behind a dam, can be used to turn water turbines to drive generators. On a much smaller scale, fuel may be burned in gas turbine engines to power generators.

Whatever the prime energy source, the electricity from a power station comes from large alternators. They produce alternating current (AC) at a frequency of 50 or 60 hertz (cycles per second), at very high currents and at voltages of a few hundred volts.

Electricity distribution

Large currents need thick conductors or they get hot and melt. To avoid using heavy cables for major transmission lines, the supply is transformed to lower currents at much higher voltages (300,000 to 400,000 volts). It is transformed down again to 33,000 or 11,000 volts for local distribution, before finally being converted to the mains voltages of 110 or 240 volts for supply to houses and industry.

The output from a power station is measured in watts (equal to the product of the current and voltage). A

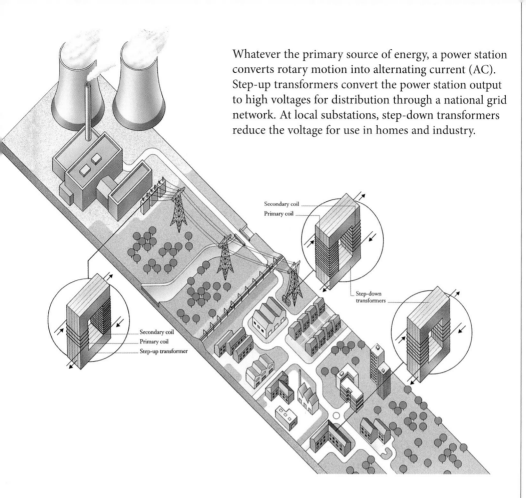

Whatever the primary source of energy, a power station converts rotary motion into alternating current (AC). Step-up transformers convert the power station output to high voltages for distribution through a national grid network. At local substations, step-down transformers reduce the voltage for use in homes and industry.

Secondary coil
Primary coil

Step-down transformers

Secondary coil
Primary coil
Step-up transformer

power station with a capacity of several hundred megawatts (million watts) can supply the needs of a small town.

Transformers

Key stages in electricity distribution rely on transformers to raise and lower voltages. A simple transformer consists of a core of soft iron wound with two overlapping coils of insulated wire. Alternating current flowing in the first, or primary, coil acts like an electromagnet to create a rapidly varying magnetic field in the core. This varying field induces an alternating current in the secondary coil.

If there are more turns of wire in the primary than in the secondary, the voltage is reduced (a step-down transformer); if the secondary turns outnumber the primary turns, the voltage is increased (step-up transformer). For any transformer, the ratio of the input voltage to the output voltage equals the ratio of the turns of wire on the primary to the turns on the secondary.

Transformers are extremely efficient, and voltage conversions take place with very little energy loss. The large currents in high-voltage transformers generate heat, and they are often bathed in oil to conduct the heat away safely.

Alternative energy sources

It is difficult to see how modern society can reduce its dependence on electric power. But because there are only limited reserves of fossil fuels, and because of the possible dangers of nuclear power and concern about nuclear waste disposal, scientists and engineers continue to investigate other ways of generating electricity. These include solar energy, wind power, and the tidal movement of water masses in the oceans.

Alternative energy sources can also have their problems. Solar power is costly and inefficient, and obviously can generate power continuously only during the hours of daylight. For these reasons it will probably continue to be reserved for places remote from other electricity supplies. Wind farms—banks of modern windmills linked directly to individual electricity generators—have attracted bad publicity because of the loud noise they also produce. The few large-scale experiments with tidal and wave power have not attracted so much environmental criticism, but the long-term effects continue to be assessed.

Curriculum Context

For many curricula, students should know that the slow speed of radioactive decay in some unstable isotopes means that they remain radioactive for many years.

Electromagnetism

A magnet made from a piece of steel is called a permanent magnet because, once magnetized, it keeps its magnetism. An electromagnet is a temporary magnet associated with a flowing electric current—turning off the current turns off the magnet.

A simple electromagnet consist of a length of iron, called the core, wrapped around and around with a length of insulated wire. When the ends of the wire are connected to a current supply such as a battery, the iron becomes magnetized and the whole arrangement acts just like a permanent magnet. It is not surprising that the branch of physics that deals with this interaction of electricity and magnetism is called electromagnetism.

History

The British scientist Michael Faraday championed this area of science in the 1830s, although the first electromagnets had been constructed a few years earlier by the American physicist Joseph Henry. There were three key stages in the scientific development of electromagnetism. The first was the 1820 observation by the Danish physicist Hans Christian Oersted that there is a magnetic field surrounding a wire carrying an electric current. He deduced this fact when he observed the deflection of a compass needle place near a current-carrying wire.

The second major step was taken about 10 years later when Faraday proved experimentally that a magnetic field that is changing induces a current in an associated circuit. The third and final stage came in the 1870s when Scottish theoretical physicist James Clerk Maxwell explained the interaction between electricity and magnetism in a set of mathematical equations. He showed that a changing electric field should produce a magnetic field and predicted the existence of

> **Curriculum Context**
>
> For many curricula, students should know that electricity and magnetism are known to be two manifestations of a single phenomenon, the electromagnetic force. The originally separate theories explaining electricity and magnetism have been combined into a single theory of electromagnetism.

electromagnetic waves that travel at the speed of light. Indeed light is such a wave, as are radio waves and all the other types of electromagnetic radiation discovered after Maxwell's time.

Uses of electromagnets

Simple electromagnets have limited uses, perhaps the best-known being to lift pieces of iron and steel in a scrap yard. This application demonstrates one of the great advantages of an electromagnet: it can be on to pick up scrap and then off again to dump it.

Other applications of electromagnets include dynamos, electric motors, electric bells, solenoids, and relays. A solenoid is a simple switching device, consisting of a sliding, spring-loaded electromagnet. Its movement is commonly used for opening and closing the contacts in a relay (a type of high-voltage switch).

Electromagnets are also key components in some kinds of microphones, loudspeakers and audio and video tape decks. MRI scanners and particle accelerators use some of the most powerful electromagnets in the world.

Maglev (magnetic levitation) trains have superconducting magnets in the body of the train. Repulsion between these and electromagnets on the track make the train "float", and attractive forces propel it along the track. This maglev in Shanghai can reach speeds of 270 mph (431 km/h).

MRI scanner

MRI stands for magnetic resonance imaging. MRI scanners can produce images of the organs inside the body. They are used in medical diagnosis. Unlike X-rays they show soft tissue better than bones.

Electric Motors

The simplest electric machines use electrical energy to do useful work, usually by converting it to mechanical energy. In electric motors, the interaction of magnetic and electric fields produces rotary motion.

A simple motor

A small direct current (DC) motor has a U-shaped magnet to produce the magnetic field. In larger motors, the magnetic field is itself produced electromagnetically by current flowing through turns of wire around an iron core. The current to drive the motor flows around a coil of wire, which is mounted so that it can rotate in the magnetic field. The current enters the coil through a split ring of metal called a commutator. For an extremely simple motor with only a single turn of wire in its coil, the commutator has two segments, each connected to wires leading to or from the coil. Practical motors have many coils forming an armature, and they need a correspondingly larger number of segments in the commutator.

When current flows along a wire in a magnetic field, the wire moves. When current flows around the coil in a motor, it rotates. After part of a turn, the commutator reverses the direction of current flow in the coil, with the result that it keeps rotating.

AC motors

With alternating current (AC), the direction of the current changes continuously and rapidly. For this reason, an AC motor does not need a segmented commutator. But to start the armature turning—and to make sure it turns in the required direction—commercial AC motors have an extra stationary coil. In combination with the windings used to create the motor's magnetic field, the stationary coil creates a secondary magnetic field. This field rotates, pulling the armature around with it.

Armature

The central, rotating part of an electric motor, usually consisting of several wire coils wound at different angles.

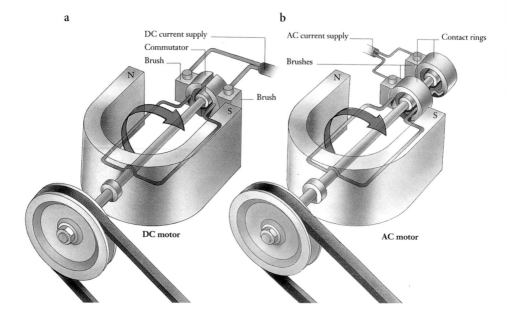

a

DC current supply
Commutator
Brush
N
S
Brush
DC motor

b

AC current supply
Brushes
N
S
Contact rings
AC motor

(a) In a simple DC motor, the current passes through a commutator with two segments. The commutator reverses the direction of the current each half turn, to keep the coil spinning within the magnetic field in the same direction. (b) The AC motor does not need a commutator, as the direction of the alternating current changes 50 or 60 times a second.

The most common type of small AC motor—an induction motor—has no commutator at all. The armature coils are replaced by a set of bars of aluminum or copper joined at each end to a metal ring and embedded in a cylinder of iron. This arrangement forms the armature and, because of its shape, it is called a squirrel cage. A series of stationary coils mounted cylindrically around the armature—called field windings—create a magnetic field which cuts the cage's metal bars and induces a current in them. This current causes the turning effect common to all electric motors, and the armature rotates inside the outer windings, or stator.

Linear motors
Similar field windings can be incorporated into a long flat stator, and the squirrel cage rotor can also be

Stator
The outer, stationary part of an electric motor. This may consist of a permanent magnet or a series of electromagnetic coils.

c

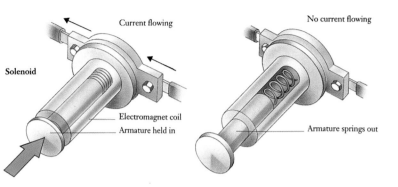

Current flowing

No current flowing

Solenoid

Electromagnet coil
Armature held in

Armature springs out

(c) A solenoid is a sliding, spring-loaded electro-magnet. When current flows in the coil surrounding the armature, the iron is held back magnetically against the tension of the spring. When the current is turned off, the armature springs out.

"opened out" to form a flat armature resting on it. When an AC current flows in the stator, the armature moves sideways, producing a linear motor. Such motors are used on a small scale to move sliding doors, and on a large scale can power a fast, silent linear motor train.

Solenoids

A simpler device—a solenoid—also uses electric current to produce sideways movement. It consists of a cylindrical coil of wire, which behaves like a bar magnet when current flows in it. There is a piece of iron (also called an armature) along the axis of the coil and, when the current is switched on, the magnetic field moves the iron sideways. The moving armature can strike the chimes of an electric doorbell, or open and close the contacts of a switch. In this way, a small current can be made to switch a much larger one, and solenoids are common in switch gear for controlling high currents.

Electrolysis

In a battery, chemical energy is converted into electrical energy—a chemical reaction generates electric current. Conversely, electricity can be used to bring about a chemical reaction. This is the principle underlying electrolysis.

Decomposition of water

A simple example is the electrolysis of water (containing a small quantity of an acid to make it a better conductor). If two electrodes are dipped into acidified water and a battery is connected between them, bubbles of gas form on the electrodes. Water is a compound of hydrogen and oxygen with the formula H_2O. The electricity has the effect of splitting the water molecules in two, so that hydrogen and oxygen gases are evolved at the electrodes.

Many other substances can be decomposed in a similar way by electrolysis, particularly salts in solution or in the molten state. This is because molten salts and solutions of salts are dissociated into ions, which are charged either positively or negatively. The amount of a substance released during electrolysis depends on the quantity of electricity used. This relationship is one of Faraday's laws of electrolysis, named for their discoverer Michael Faraday (1791–1867).

Extraction of elements

Electrolysis is one of the most important commercial applications of electricity, after power and light. Two major industrial applications of electrolysis are in the extraction of elements from their compounds and in electroplating. Chlorine gas is manufactured by the electrolysis of sea water or a solution of common salt (sodium chloride, NaCl). Pure copper is produced by the electrolysis of a solution of copper salts, and reactive metals such as aluminum and magnesium are obtained by electrolysis of their molten ores.

Electrode

A conductor used as the positive or negative terminal through which electric current passes between metallic and nonmetallic parts of an electric circuit.

These climbing karabiners have an anodized aluminum surface. Different dyes have been used to anodize them in different colors.

Electroplating

In most electroplating, the object to be plated is made the cathode of an electrolytic cell. The electrolyte contains a salt of the plating metal. When current flows through the cell, ions of the metal travel to the cathode, become discharged, and are deposited as a coat upon the object to be plated. Electroplating is commonly employed for protective and decorative finishes, using metals such as chromium, copper, nickel, silver, and gold.

In some applications the object to be treated is placed at the anode of the cell. For example, if an object made of aluminum or one of its alloys is made the anode (positive electrode) in an electrolyte consisting of a strong alkali such as caustic soda (sodium hydroxide), the object is given a thin, adherent coat of oxide. This process is called anodizing. The oxide layer protects the metal against abrasion and corrosion and, because of its chemical nature, can also be dyed or printed. Steel and various copper alloys such as brass and bronze can also be anodized in order to give them decorative finishes.

Anode
A positive electrode.

Cathode
A negative electrode.

Anion
A negative ion.

Cation
A positive ion.

Electricity and Other Energy

Because various forms of energy can be changed into each other, electricity can be generated directly from light or heat. It can even be produced from mechanical energy, without the use of electromagnetism as in a dynamo or alternator.

Ammeter

An instrument for measuring the flow of electric current in a circuit.

Doping

The process of introducing impurities into an extremely pure semiconductor to change its electrical properties.

The photoelectric effect

When light or other kinds of electromagnetic radiation such as ultraviolet or X-rays shine onto a metal, electrons are emitted from its surface. If the metal is connected into an external circuit, an electric current flows. The photoelectric effect arises when the incoming light has enough energy—that is, it is of a high enough frequency—to knock electrons out of the metal's atoms. Some metals, for example selenium, are more photosensitive than others.

The photoelectric effect is put to very good use in photocells and solar panels. A photographer's exposure meter, for example, may contain a selenium photocell and a sensitive ammeter. The brighter the light, the greater the current produced. Most solar panels use photoresistors or photovoltaic cells made of a semiconductor such as silicon that has been doped to increase the its photoelectric effect. Electricity made this way is expensive, but is useful for applications such as spacecraft. Solar panels are also employed in sunny climates to generate electricity. They are particularly useful far from an electricity supply.

The Seebeck effect

Thermoelectricity—generating electricity by heat—is produced by joining two wires of different metals to form a loop, and keeping the junctions at different temperatures. Called the Seebeck effect, after the German physicist Thomas Seebeck (1770–1831), it arises because electrons exist at different energy levels in the atoms of the dissimilar metals. At the junctions,

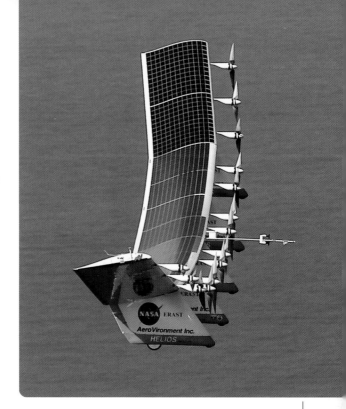

Helios was a prototype remote-controlled solar-powered aircraft that was developed by NASA in 1999. The 245-foot (75-m) wingspan was covered with more than 65,000 solar cells.

electrons flow from one metal to the other. The greater the temperature difference between the junctions, the greater the current flow. By keeping one junction at a known temperature, the effect can be used to make a thermometer for measuring the temperature at the other junction.

The thermionic effect

When current passes through a wire in a vacuum, the wire gets hot and gives off streams of electrons. Called the thermionic effect, this is the source of electrons in a thermionic valve (vacuum tube) or cathode-ray tube, which often has a heated cathode, with a stream of electrons flowing to an anode.

The piezoelectric effect

The piezoelectric effect occurs when certain crystals (for example quartz) are subject to mechanical strain. The force acting on the crystal generates a small electric current. Opposite faces of the deformed crystal acquire opposite electric charges, resulting in a flow of electrons. Piezoelectric crystals are used in "electronic" cigarette lighters, in which the current generated causes a spark to ignite the gas. They are also used in strain gages, microbalances, and in pickups (contact microphones) for amplifying instruments such as guitars. Crystals are also used in clocks and watches to generate a rapid, constant electric pulse.

Alternative Energy Sources

All the energy we use on Earth—except nuclear power—comes ultimately from the Sun. Wood that some people burn for heating and cooking comes from trees that use the energy of the Sun in photosynthesis to build up their tissues. Fossil fuels such as coal, oil, and gas derive from plants and other organisms that used sunlight millions of years ago. Currently 80 percent of the energy we use comes from fossil fuels.

Fossil fuels are finite sources of energy and will one day be used up. They are also the main source of atmospheric carbon dioxide and a major cause of climate change. Scientists and engineers around the world are working on the development and improvement of renewable energy sources that can eventually replace fossil fuels.

Hydroelectricity and solar power

About 7 percent of the world's energy consumption comes from hydroelectricity—electricity generated by flowing water, generally from behind a dam. Although "renewable" (as long as it continues to rain), this energy relies on suitable places to site the dams. It is not an option for a dry country with no mountains or dammable valleys. Also dams can have a devastating effect on the local plants and animals, both above and below the dam.

Every day during daylight hours, each square kilometer of the Earth's surface receives about 4000 megawatts of energy from the Sun. This amount of power—4000 million watts – is enough for the needs of a small town. If only we could "catch" some of this solar energy; but photocells and other devices for converting sunlight into electricity are inefficient and very expensive. At present the best way is to let plants use the energy, then burn the plants.

Wind and wave power

Wind power is another alternative that has been used since ancient times. Wind powered the first ocean-going ships, and windmills drove machines to grind corn or pump water for irrigation. Today's wind turbines are more efficient and convert wind power directly into electricity. Arrays of turbines on a wind farm can generate enough electricity for a small town, although nearby residents often complain about the noise they make. The United States alone has nearly 20,000 wind turbines in regular use.

In conjunction with the Moon, the Sun has another energetic effect on Earth; the combined gravitational pull of these two bodies causes the twice-daily regular rise and fall of the tides. Experiments with harnessing the tides continue in an attempt to find a non-polluting alternative source of energy.

Nuclear energy

Nuclear power is declining in popularity as a source of energy, partly as a result of some nearly disastrous accidents but mainly because of the difficulty of disposing of spent nuclear fuel and decommissioning

Curriculum Context

For most curricula, students are expected to be able to rate the environmental advantages and disadvantages of heating a home with electricity, natural gas (or propane), solar power, oil, or coal.

Wave power is still in the early stages of development, but this onshore design has been successful on a small scale. An incoming wave forces air along a channel where it turns a turbine. As the wave retreats, it sucks air back through the turbine, which rotates in the opposite direction. The turbine drives an electric generator.

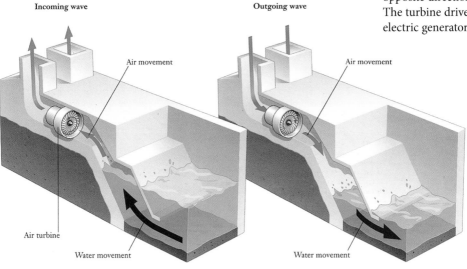

Incoming wave

Outgoing wave

Air movement

Air movement

Air turbine

Water movement

Water movement

old nuclear power plants. Only France still derives much of its electricity from such sources, probably because the country has few deposits of coal and oil. And apart from military submarines, nuclear-powered vessels have not been developed as once predicted.

Geothermal energy

One derivative of nuclear processes does however hold out more promise. The center of the Earth itself is heated by reactions within the Earth's interior. Geysers and hot springs are natural manifestations of this geothermal power, which can also be harnessed by drilling boreholes into layers of hot rock, which can reach temperatures of up to 350°C, and pumping in cold water. The boiling hot water flows up another borehole and can be used for driving steam turbines, and also for direct heating of nearby homes and other buildings. Differences in temperature and salinity between different water levels in the oceans have also been "tapped" as experimental sources of energy.

In the United States, geysers to the north of San Francisco have been harnessed in this way, although the earliest people to make use of this "free" energy were the people of Larderello, Italy, who had a geothermal steam-powered generator as long ago as 1904. The biggest geothermal energy producers are China, the USA, Iceland, and Turkey.

Other energy sources

Other possible energy sources—at least theoretically—include chemical energy, as exploited in batteries and in experimental fuel cells. At present, weight and expense preclude these from being viable. Trash and other waste products can be made to produce chemical energy, either by controlled burning or by the fermentation of biomass to produce fuel gases such as methane.

Electronics and Semiconductors

Some unusual ways of generating electricity involve the flow of electrons in a vacuum and in solids other than metals. Electronic devices—as they are known—are used to switch and control the flow of currents carrying information, such as sound signals in an amplifier or the digital data signals in a computer.

Vacuum tubes

The first electronic devices were vacuum tubes or valves, in which a stream of electrons (electric current) flowed from a heated cathode to an anode. A two-electrode vacuum tube, or diode, allowed current to flow in one direction but not the other. This is useful for changing AC into DC. Adding a third electrode, or grid, makes a triode, which can be used for controlling and amplifying current.

However, vacuum tubes are bulky and their heaters consume power. In the years following World War II, scientists in the United States invented the transistor, a solid-state device equivalent to the triode. The term solid state means that the electrons travel only in solid substances, not a gas or a vacuum. A transistor consumes no power and can be made extremely small.

Semiconduting materials

A semiconductor is a material that has an electric resistance less than an insulator but greater than a conductor. A metal has many free electrons in its structure that can conduct current; an insulator has hardly any. Semiconductors, such as germanium and silicon have some free electrons, which can act as current carriers. Both of these elements have four outer electrons in their atoms. The addition of a very small amount of another element with five outer electrons, such as phosphorous—a process called doping—provides extra conducting electrons, creating an n-type

Cathode
A negative electrode.

Anode
A positive electrode.

Curriculum Context

For many curricula, students should understand the properties of transistors and the role of transistors in electric circuits.

semiconductor. Doping with an element with three outer electrons, such as boron, leaves some atoms with a deficiency of electrons (called holes), into which free electrons can flow. The resulting material is called a p-type semiconductor.

Diodes and Transistors

Joining a piece of n-type semiconductor to a piece of p-type semiconductor creates a diode. Free electrons from the n-type flow across the junction to occupy holes in the p-type, but cannot flow from the p-type to the n-type. Two junction diodes back to back (an n-p-n or p-n-p arrangement) form a transistor. A small current fed to the middle piece (the base) controls a larger current between the outer pieces (the emitter and the collector). In a field-effect transistor, one type of semiconductor (the gate) is diffused into the sides of a rod of the other type. The main current is fed between the ends of the rod (at the source and the drain). A smaller varying current supplied to the gate controls the main current as the base current controls the emitter in a junction transistor. A transistor can act as an amplifier or as a very fast electronic switch.

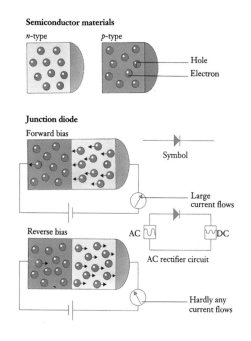

Semiconductor materials

n-type p-type

Hole
Electron

Junction diode

Forward bias

Symbol

Large current flows

Reverse bias   AC   DC

AC rectifier circuit

Hardly any current flows

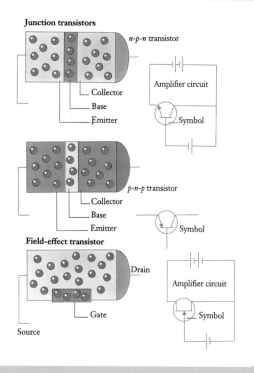

Junction transistors

n-p-n transistor

Collector
Base
Emitter

Amplifier circuit

Symbol

p-n-p transistor

Collector
Base
Emitter

Symbol

Field-effect transistor

Drain

Amplifier circuit

Gate

Symbol

Source

Producing Sounds

Sound is a form of energy that originates when something vibrates—such as a guitar string, the human vocal cords, or the reed in the mouthpiece of a saxophone. The vibrations cause waves of alternate high pressure (compression) and low pressure (rarefaction) in the molecules of the air.

Sound waves travel out in all directions from their source at a speed of 334 meters per second in dry air. They also travel in other mediums, such as water and solid. The denser the medium, the faster they travel. If there is no medium to carry them, sound waves cannot move; sound will not travel through a vacuum.

Curriculum Context

For most curricula, students should know that sound waves and most other waves occur only in matter.

Wavelength, frequency, and intensity

Like all forms of wave motion, sound has wavelength—the distance between the crests (or troughs) of consecutive waves. The number of waves generated each second is its frequency, typically between 20 and 20,000 hertz (cycles per second) in the range audible to humans. Frequency of a pure tone is a measure of its pitch. The amplitude of a sound wave is its height above mean level and is a measure of intensity.

Intensity is not exactly the same as loudness, because the loudness of sound depends also on its frequency. Loudness is a measure of the amount of sound power that passes through a particular area each second. This is measured in decibels.

Producing sound

From an engine rattle in a car to the whistling of a draft through a window, sound is produced by vibrations. Musical instruments make use of this fact. In a percussion instrument such as a drum or a cymbal, a plastic skin or thin sheet of metal vibrates and generates sound when struck.

Vibrating strings

In a violin and similar stringed instruments, sound is generated when the strings are kept vibrating by the action of a bow. The body of a violin or guitar acts as a resonator, vibrating at the same frequency as the basic tone generated by the string and so amplifying it. The shape of the body ensures that it resonates at most frequencies within its range.

The pitch (frequency) of a vibrating string depends on three properties of the string: its thickness, its length, and its tension. A string that is thick, long,, or slack produces a lower tone than one that is thin, short, or taut. High notes on a guitar or violin are played on the thinner strings. To get even higher notes, a guitarist (or violinist) presses the string to the fingerboard, making the string shorter. The change in pitch with tension can be heard when a string player tunes the instrument by increasing or decreasing the tightness of the strings.

Wind instruments

The sound from a flute, trumpet, or other wind instrument comes from a vibrating column of air. The air takes the form of a "standing wave," with alternate nodes (at which the air is stationary) and antinodes (at which it has maximum vibration). Higher notes are produced by blowing harder, creating standing waves with a greater number of nodes and antinodes. Alternatively, the player can uncover holes or press valves, making the vibrating air column shorter.

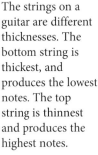

Standing wave

A stationary pattern of waves produced by two waves of the same frequency traveling in opposite directions.

The strings on a guitar are different thicknesses. The bottom string is thickest, and produces the lowest notes. The top string is thinnest and produces the highest notes.

Acoustics

When sound waves strike an obstruction, they bounce back. In a very large room or hall—such as a cathedral—sounds bounce off the walls and ceiling. This results in reverberation, in which the listener hears the same sound at several slightly different moments, depending on how far it has traveled as it bounces around. If the reflecting surface is large and more than about 30 meters away from the sound source, the reflection is heard as an echo.

Sound waves can bend around some obstructions in a process called diffraction. The direction of sound waves also changes when they travel from one medium to another of different density—an effect known as refraction.

Interference

Two sound waves of about the same frequency can combine to produce a new wave. Called interference, this phenomenon gives rise to regular variations in loudness known as beats. When the peaks of the two combining waves coincide, a louder sound is created. When the peaks of one wave coincide with the troughs of the other, the two sounds cancel each other. The number of beats heard per second equals the difference between the frequencies of the combining waves. Musicians make use of beats when tuning an instrument to a standard reference note (an orchestra tunes to the note A played on an oboe). The instrument is "in tune"—playing exactly the same A as that of the oboe—when no beats can be heard. A tuning fork—a metal implement with two prongs—may also be used to produce a standard tone to which the tuning of an instrument may be matched.

Speed of Sound

In dry air at sea level, sound travels at a speed of 747 miles per hour (334 m/s). Strange effects occur when the source of a sound is supersonic. When a supersonic jet aircraft flies overhead, the series of compressions in the air (caused by the engine noise) forms a shock wave that follows the aircraft and creates a loud bang called a sonic boom as it passes a listener.

Supersonic
Faster than the speed of sound.

The sound barrier

A sonic boom is not an isolated bang but part of a continuous noise which trails in the wake of the aircraft. The wave of compression first forms in front of the aircraft as it approaches the speed of sound, creating shock waves that caused wings of early subsonic aircraft to fail.

This "sound barrier" proved to be an obstacle for aircraft designers until it was first broken by an American rocket-powered aircraft in 1947. The sound barrier consists of a "wall" of high-pressure air caused by the buildup of sound waves, and extra force is needed to enable an aircraft to break through the barrier. The shock wave that accompanies a sonic boom also represents a sudden increase in pressure, which can be enough to damage structures on the ground in its path.

The Doppler effect

If the source of a sound moves, the frequency (pitch) of the sound is affected. When the source of sound rapidly approaches a listener, the sound waves are "squeezed" together, increasing their frequency and raising the pitch of the sound. When the source is moving away from a listener, the waves are "stretched" further apart, and the frequency and pitch fall. This phenomenon is called the Doppler effect, for the Austrian physicist Christian Doppler who first explained

it in 1842. The Doppler effect is also shown by other wave phenomena (as in Doppler radar) and by light, manifested as the red shift in the spectrum of a fast-receding star.

Ultrasound and infrasound

Ultrasound has frequencies higher than the upper limit of human hearing (about 20,000 hertz for a young adult). It has many applications in technology and nature. Sounds below the lower limit of human hearing (about 20 hertz), called subsonic or infrasound, are used in geological surveying. Engineers detonate explosives underground, and detect the infrasound waves with a series of microphones. The time taken for the waves to reach the microphones provides information about the types of rocks they traveled through, because rocks bend (refract) the sound waves. In the natural world, creatures as different as spiders and elephants can detect infrasound, and possibly use it as a means of communication.

This astonishing picture shows a US Navy F-18 Hornet just as it breaks the sound barrier. Scientists are still debating the explanation of the disk of vapor. The first person to break the sound barrier was US pilot Chuck Yeager, who in 1947 flew the Bell X-1 rocket-powered plane at a speed of over 720 mph or 1150 km/h (Mach 1).

Ultrasound

With frequencies greater than about 20,000 hertz, ultrasound is inaudible to humans. But some animals can hear and produce such frequencies. An insect-eating bat, for example, emits ultrasonic squeaks and can hear their echoes. The very high frequency of ultrasound enables the bat to use this form of echolocation to detect small objects. Some whales and dolphins also use ultrasound for navigation and for communication.

Hertz (Hz)

The unit of frquency.
1 Hz = 1 cycle per second.

Curriculum Context

For most curricula, students should know that frequency is the number of wavelengths that pass any point in space per second. A wave will make any particle it encounters move in regular cycles, and frequency is also the number of such cycles made per second.

Sonar

These natural systems are imitated by sonar (SOund Navigation And Ranging), which employs ultrasound in the frequency range 100,000 to 10 million hertz under water. Sound travels at about 1500 meters per second in water, more than four times as fast as in air. It is transmitted by a transducer (similar in principle to a loudspeaker) and detected by directional hydrophones (similar to microphones). The direction of an echo gives an indication of a target's bearing, and the time taken for the sound signals to travel out and back can be used to calculate its range, or distance. The range equals a quarter of the speed of sound (in water) multiplied by the time the ultrasound pulses take to travel to the target and back. The bearing and range are displayed on a television-type screen, or processed by a computer.

Echo-sounding

A simple application of sonar is echo sounding, in which the time taken for sound to be reflected back to a vessel from the bottom of the sea is used to calculate the depth of water below its keel. Commercial fishermen use similar devices called fish finders to locate shoals of fish by their sonar echoes; it is type of echolocation. A more sophisticated device is a side-scan sonar. It sends a pulsed narrow beam of ultrasonic signals at right angles to the course of the ship. Any

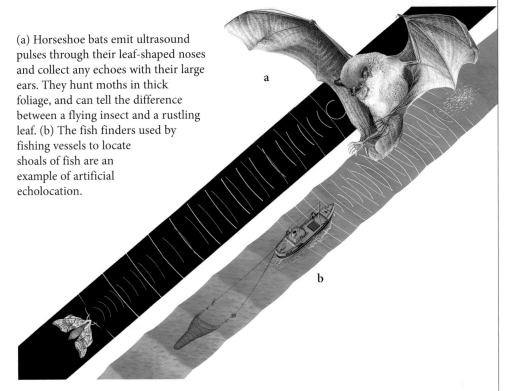

(a) Horseshoe bats emit ultrasound pulses through their leaf-shaped noses and collect any echoes with their large ears. They hunt moths in thick foliage, and can tell the difference between a flying insect and a rustling leaf. (b) The fish finders used by fishing vessels to locate shoals of fish are an example of artificial echolocation.

echoes are computer-processed line by line to build up a "picture" of the object that is causing the reflections.

Ultrasound applications

Scanning with ultrasound also has various medical applications, in which it is valued as a harmless, non-invasive technique for investigating structures within the body. In Western countries, pregnant women routinely have ultrasonic scans of the uterus to check on the progress of the developing fetus. Other organs that can be scanned include the brain and the heart.

Engineers employ ultrasonic probes to detect flaws in castings and welded joints. The echoes reflected from within the structure are converted into signals that can be displayed on a computer screen, to reveal the location of any holes or defects. Ultrasonic echoes are also used by farmers to measure the thickness of fat on animals raised for meat. In industry, ultrasonic cleaning is used to remove all traces of grease from components, particularly before electroplating.

Infrasound

Infrasound is sound that is too low in pitch for humans to hear, that is with frequencies less than about 20 hertz. Infrasound can be heard by some animals, however. Using infrasound, elephants can communicate at a distance of 2.5 miles (4 km), and hunting spiders can listen for the footfalls of their approaching prey.

Seismic waves

Like all forms of sound, infrasound must have a medium in which to travel. Very low-frequency sounds can be "felt" by humans as vibrations, such as the sensation associated with high-speed machinery or the tremors that accompany Earth movements caused by active faults or earthquakes. Earthquake waves—called seismic waves—travel through the Earth or along the surface from the site (focus) of an earthquake. They can be detected and recorded by seismographs.

The amplitude of a wave is an indication of its strength and is the basis of the Richter scale for measuring earthquake intensity. The Richter scale was devised by the American geologist Charles Richter in 1935. The alternative Mercalli scale, named in 1931 for Italian geologist Giuseppe Mercalli, is based on the damage caused.

Curriculum Context

For most curricula, students should be able to identify transverse and longitudinal waves in mechanical media, such as S and P seismic waves.

There are three main types of seismic waves. S waves (shear waves) vibrate the rock at right angles to the direction the wave travels in. P waves (primary waves) move along as waves of compression within the rock, like sound waves traveling through air. And L waves (long waves) travel along the surface with an up and down motion, like ripples on water.

Seismographs

There are two main types of seismographs, which both rely on the inertia of a heavy mass of metal. When the ground shakes in an earthquake, inertia makes the metallic mass tend to remain still while the rest of the apparatus vibrates, either up and down or from side to side. A pen attached to the metallic mass draws a trace on paper attached to a rotating drum to make a permanent record of any seismic activity.

Studying rock structure

Seismic waves move at different speeds in rocks of different density. Geologists and prospectors make use of this fact to study the structure of rocks. They bore a hole and detonate an explosive charge at the bottom of it. A series of seismographs pick up the resulting waves, whose pattern can reveal the presence of any unusual formations, such as underground deposits of minerals (particularly oil). Similar seismographs are also used to detect the explosion of nuclear devices underground anywhere in the world.

Hunting spiders like this wolf spider have hearing organs on their legs that can pick up infrasound waves produced by the movement of other creatures.

Producing Light

Light is a type of energy that powers all life on Earth. Plants use light from the Sun to build their tissues, and animals—including humans—eat plants or animals that have eaten plants. Every living organism is therefore dependent on light. Light also enables us to see color in the world around us.

Electromagnetic radiation

Like radio waves and X rays, light is a form of electromagnetic energy. All are produced by the activity of electrons in atoms. When some of the electrons in an atom become energized and then lose energy, the electrons "jump" from one energy level to a lower one. The energy difference is given off as radiation—either forms that can be seen (visible light), or beyond the visible spectrum, like infrared, ultraviolet, radio waves, and X rays.

Also, like other forms of electromagnetic radiation, light can be described in terms of its frequency and wavelength. Frequency is the number of waves that are generated each second. Wavelength is the distance between successive peaks (or troughs) of a wave.

To the human eye, different light wavelengths appear as different colors. The shorter wavelengths are violet or blue; the longer wavelengths appear as red light. The whole range of visible wavelengths can be seen in a spectrum, which is produced naturally in a rainbow or in the laboratory by passing light through a glass prism.

Producing light

All devices for producing light, from a candle or electric lamp to a fluorescent tube or laser, depend on processes that take place within atoms. All of these processes involve electrons.

In a neutral atom, the electrons occupy different orbits representing different levels of energy: the orbit closest to the nucleus has low energy, while the outer orbits have higher energy. Extra energy supplied to the atom—by heating it, for instance—is absorbed by the electrons and causes them to "jump" to higher energy levels. However, they are unstable in this excited state, and quickly jump back to their original levels. As they do, the extra energy they have absorbed is emitted as light. The wavelength (and therefore the color) of the emitted light varies depending on what element is being used.

Light can be produced in various ways. The chief difference is in the way the extra energy is supplied to the atom. In the flame of a candle or oil lamp, carbon from the hydrocarbons in the wax or oil is heated until it glows. Heat is also the energy source for light from a gas lamp, which has a mantle—a sheath placed around the flame. Atoms of thorium metal in the mantle give off an intense white light.

Electric light

In an ordinary electric lightbulb, the heat is produced when electric current flows through the thin tungsten wire of the filament; the tungsten atoms give off light. In an electric arc lamp, the very intense light comes from a white-hot spark as it jumps between two carbon electrodes.

Another way of converting electron energy into light energy—without involving heat—occurs in a discharge tube, such as the type used for neon advertising signs. The tubes contain traces of neon gas at low pressure. Electric current flowing into an electrode (cathode) at one end of the tube produces a stream of electrons. As these flow along the tube to the electrode (anode) at the other end, they collide with neon atoms, exciting some of their electrons to a

Curriculum Context

For most curricula, students should know that the energy of each electron in an atom keeps it in motion around the positive nucleus to which it is attracted. The structure of multielectron atoms is understood in terms of electrons filling energy levels that define orbitals.

higher energy level. When the excited electrons return to their original level, the familiar red neon light is emitted. The use of the gas xenon instead of neon gives a tube that produces the bright white light of a photographer's electronic flash.

Fluorescent light

A fluorescent tube is a slightly different source of unheated (or "cold") electric light. Like a discharge tube, the fluorescent tube also involves an electric current and two electrodes, but in this case the gas used in the tube is mercury vapor at low pressure, which produces invisible ultraviolet light. The inside of the fluorescent tube is coated with a substance called a phosphor. As the phospohor is struck by ultraviolet light, some of its atoms are excited. When they return to their normal stable state, they give off visible light. Different types of phosphors produce light of different colors.

Phosphors are fluorescent, which means that they stop emitting light after the supply of stimulating radiation (whether ultraviolet light or electron streams) is stopped. A similar phenomenon is known as phosphorescence. In this case, however, the light continues to be emitted for a short time after the stimulating radiation stops. This is how phosphorescent substances such as luminous paints—which absorb sunlight—glow in the dark.

LEDs (light-emitting diodes) are semiconductor materials that emit light when electricity passes through them. The first LEDs were red, and were used mainly for indicator lights. However, LEDs are now more powerful and come in most colors. They may soon replace both incandescent and fluorescent lights, because they are far more efficient.

Reflection and Mirrors

Light generally travels in straight lines. In the branch of physics called optics, which is concerned with the behavior of light through mirrors, lenses, and optical instruments, light is often thought of as rays represented by straight lines. Straight rays from a light source such as the Sun or an electric lamp cause an object to cast well-defined shadows.

Plane reflection

When light rays strike an object, some of them are reflected; it is the reflected rays that enter our eyes and allow us to see the object. Some materials reflect light better than others. A perfectly black object reflects hardly any light; a highly polished piece of metal reflects nearly all the light rays that strike it. The best reflectors are mirrors, which are usually made by applying a thin coating of silver to a sheet of glass.

If a ray of light strikes a plane (flat) mirror at right angles, it is reflected back along the same path, called the normal to the mirror. Light striking a mirror at an angle to the normal is reflected at the same angle on the other side of the normal. A law of reflection of light states that the angle of incidence (between the incoming ray and the normal) equals the angle of reflection (between the reflected ray and the normal).

When rays reflected from a mirror reach our eyes, we see an image of an object that appears to be behind the mirror. This is called a virtual image, and it is the same distance behind the mirror as the object is in front of it.

Curved mirrors

Curved mirrors can be either convex (domed outward toward the viewer) or concave (domed inward, like a saucer). A point on the axis of the mirror at its radius is

One major application of curved mirrors is in astronomical telescopes. Mirrors are lighter in weight than lenses, and can be made in sections to make installation easier. This picture shows the final inspection of one section of the mirror for the James Webb space telescope, due to be launched in 2010.

called the center of curvature; half way between the center of curvature and the mirror is the point called the focus. Light rays reflected in a convex mirror form a virtual image behind the mirror; the image is smaller than the actual object. Convex mirrors are used as driving mirrors in cars and trucks.

The image formed by a concave mirror depends on the position of the object in relation to the center of curvature and focus. If the object is between the focus and the mirror, a large virtual image is formed behind the mirror. as in a curved mirror used when shaving or putting on makeup. If the object is at the focus, the virtual image is formed an infinite distance behind the mirror, and cannot be seen. When the object is outside the focus of a concave mirror, it produces a real image (so called because the image can be formed and seen on a screen, which is impossible with a virtual image). For an object located outside the center of curvature, the image is upside-down and smaller than life size. But if the object is between the focus and center of curvature, it produces a magnified, upside-down real image.

Refraction and Lenses

When a ray of light passes from one transparent medium to another of different optical density—for example from air to glass—it does not continue to travel in a straight line. On entering the denser medium, the ray is bent away from the normal in the phenomenon called refraction. The amount of refraction depends on the optical densities of the mediums.

Snell's law

The exact behavior of the light ray obeys a law formulated by the Dutch mathematician and physicist Willebrod van Roijen (1591–1626), who adopted the Latin name Snellius. Snell's law, as it is now known, states that for a light ray of a particular wavelength (color), the sine of the angle of incidence (between the incident ray and the normal) divided by the sine of the angle of refraction is a constant. This constant is the refractive index for the mediums concerned. For example, the refractive index of water is 1.5, and that of crown glass (used in camera lenses) is about 1.3.

Light travels more slowly in a dense medium. Another definition of refractive index equates it to the speed of light in a vacuum divided by the speed of light in the medium concerned. The refractive index of air is virtually the same as that of a vacuum, which is assumed to be 1.

Lens types

Refractive indices are important in the design and behavior of lenses. There are two basic types of lenses, convex and concave. A convex lens is thicker in the middle (like a magnifying glass) and a concave lens is thicker at the edges (like the lenses in glasses for nearsightedness). Light passing through the exact center—along the axis—of either lens passes right through in a straight line. But light entering a convex

Normal
The normal is a line at right angles to a plane or surface.

Sine
The sine of an angle in a right-angled triangle is the ratio of the length of the opposite side to the length of the hypotenuse (the longest side).

Curriculum Context
For many curricula, students should understand that refraction describes a change in the direction of a wave that occurs when the wave encounters a boundary between one medium and another.

lens off its axis is refracted (bent) toward the axis, and refracted again on leaving the lens; thus rays parallel to the axis are brought together at a focus behind the lens. A concave lens refracts light rays away from the axis. Rays parallel to the axis diverge after passing through the lens, and can be regarded as coming from a focus that is on the same side of the lens as the incoming light.

Because of these differences in basic behavior, convex lenses are also known as converging, or positive, lenses, and concave lenses are also called diverging, or negative, lenses. Convex lenses can form real or virtual images, depending on the position of the object in relation to the focus of the lens. Concave lenses always produce virtual images.

Chromatic aberration

The amount a ray of light is refracted by a lens depends on the color, or wavelength, of the light. For example, long-wavelength red light is refracted less than shorter-wavelength blue light. As a result, when white light (which is a mixture of all colors) passes through a simple convex lens, its red component is focused slightly farther from the lens than the blue component. An image formed by the lens has colored fringes around its edges, in the phenomenon known as chromatic aberration. This defect is overcome in high-quality lenses by making them of several components, using two types of glass to cancel out the aberration.

Optical devices

Many optical devices make use of lenses. Perhaps the most familiar, apart from the eye, is a camera, in which a convex lens—or a combination of lenses that behave overall like a positive lens—focuses a reduced, upside-down image onto the film. Simple telescopes (sometimes called terrestrial telescopes), binoculars and opera glasses use pairs of lenses to produce

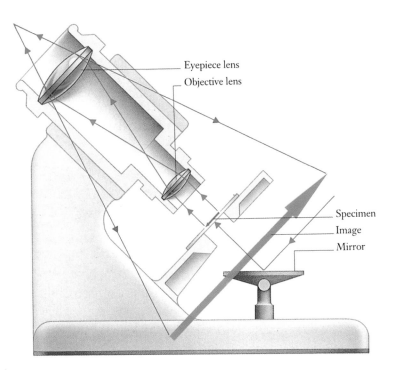

Eyepiece lens
Objective lens
Specimen
Image
Mirror

In a compound microscope, the objective lens produces an enlarged image of the specimen, which is further magnified by the eyepiece. The overall magnification is the magnifying power of the objective multiplied by the power of the eyepiece.

magnified images. Greater magnification still is produced by optical microscopes, using a combination of positive lenses.

Lenses and eyes

The lens in the eye is a convex lens, which brings images of objects to a focus on the light-sensitive retina at the back of the eye. The image is upside-down, but the brain turns it right way up. A person whose eyeball is slightly too short from front to back is farsighted (hypertropic) because the eye lens tries to focus the light rays behind the retina. The condition can be corrected by wearing eyeglasses with convex lenses. If the eyeball is too long, however, the result is nearsightedness (myopia), because light is focused in front of the retina. It can be corrected with eyeglasses having concave lenses.

Dispersion and Diffraction

When white light passes through a glass prism, its different wavelengths are bent to different extents, both on entering the prism and on leaving it. As a result, the component wavelengths are spread out to form a spectrum ranging from violet through blue, green, and yellow to orange and red. This phenomenon of spectrum formation is called dispersion. Its most familiar natural example occurs in a rainbow, which forms when sunlight is dispersed and reflected by airborne droplets of rainwater.

Curriculum Context

For most curricula, students should understand that diffraction describes the constructive and destructive patterns of waves created at the edges of objects, and that diffraction can cause waves to bend around an obstacle or to spread as they pass through an aperture.

Diffraction

Light rays are also bent when they pass through a very narrow slit. But in this effect, called diffraction, red light is bent more than blue light. A useful laboratory tool called a diffraction grating consists of a glass plate ruled with very fine lines spaced 5,000 to 10,000 per centimeter. When a beam of white light is passed through such a grating, it is split into a spectrum. If physicists, astronomers, or chemists wish to analyze the spectrum of a particular light source, they use diffraction gratings rather than prisms to create the spectrum.

Interference

Other interesting phenomena are possible when light passes through narrow slits. If monochromatic light—that is, light of a single wavelength or color—passes through a pair of slits, diffraction causes the rays to spread from each slit at all angles. Each of the rays has to travel a different distance from the slits to a screen placed beyond them.

If the lengths of the paths traveled by two rays differ by a whole number of wavelengths, they arrive at the screen "in step." They therefore reinforce each other and produce a bright line on the screen. Rays that are out of step cancel each other out in the phenomenon

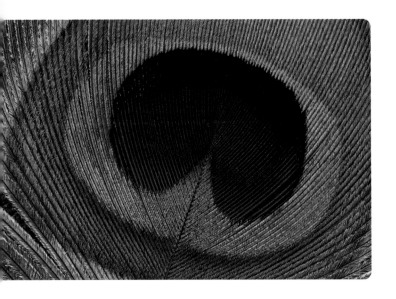

The iridescent colors of a peacock's feathers have little to do with colored pigments. The minute barbules that make up each feather cause interference patterns in the light reflected from the feather surface. The colors seem to shimmer because the wavelengths of light reaching the eye change with the angle at which the feathers are viewed.

called interference, resulting in a dark band on the screen. The pattern of light and dark bands formed in this way are called interference fringes. They can be produced in various other ways when light waves are made to travel in and out of step. For instance, a thin film of air trapped between two pieces of glass causes interference when light rays reflected from surfaces at the upper and lower edges of the film differ in path lengths. Concentric fringes produced in this way are called Newton's rings.

Interference also occurs with white light. But in this case the various wavelengths or colors are affected individually, resulting in fringes consisting of all the colors of the rainbow. Light reflected from the upper and lower surfaces of a thin film of oil on water gives rise to colored fringes in this way. The color comes from an optical effect, not from the oil itself.

A similar effect can be seen in soap bubbles, and in the light reflected from the microscopic pits on the surface of a compact disk. It can also been seen in the light reflected from the scales or feathers on the wings of some butterflies and birds.

Curriculum Context

For most curricula, students should understand that two or more waves can occupy the same region of space at the same time. The crest of one wave can overlap the crest of another, producing constructive interference, or the crest of one wave can overlap the trough of another, giving destructive interference.

Light from Lasers

A laser is a device that uses a standard light source to stimulate atoms to produce coherent light (with all the light waves in step); the term laser comes from the initial letters of Light Amplification by Stimulated Emission of Radiation.

Producing laser light

A simple laser may be based on a cylindrical crystal of ruby, which is silvered at one end to form a mirror. The other end of the crystal is semisilvered or has a central hole, so that it reflects some light and lets some light through.

A flash tube, similar to that in a photographer's flash gun, is coiled around the crystal. When it flashes, its light "excites" some of the atoms in the ruby, causing electrons in the atoms to jump to a much higher energy level. When the flash tube is off, the electrons revert to a lower energy level, but one that is still higher than the original level. Further absorption of light energy by

With the initial flash of intense light from the flash tube, some of the electrons in the laser's ruby atoms are excited to a high energy level. These electrons then revert to a lower (but still higher than normal) level. At the next flash, they briefly absorb more light and then emit it as coherent laser light when they return to their normal level.

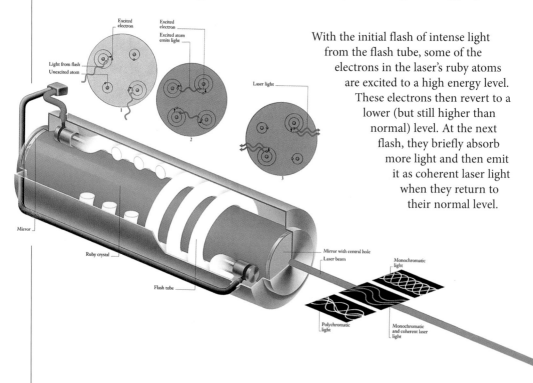

Excited electron
Excited electron
Excited atom emits light
Light from flash
Unexcited atom
Laser light
1
2
3
Mirror
Ruby crystal
Mirror with central hole
Laser beam
Monochromatic light
Flash tube
Polychromatic light
Monochromatic and coherent laser light

these atoms causes them to emit laser light as the electrons finally return to their original level.

This light is reflected back and forth within the crystal, continuing to stimulate more and more ruby atoms to emit light, while some of it emerges as a pulse of laser light through the semisilvered mirror, or through the hole in one mirror. The ruby laser can produce only short bursts of laser light, but lasers using carbon dioxide or other gases produce continuous laser light, and the gas atoms can be excited by high-frequency radio waves instead of flashes of light.

Laser applications

Lasers have been used in many applications since they were first produced in the 1960s. In medicine, a laser beam can be used like a fine scalpel to remove skin blemishes and small growths, cauterize broken blood vessels and tack back a detached retina in the eye. Laser beams can be introduced into body cavities along optical fibers. Fiber optics and lasers are also used in telecommunications. Infrared laser beams passing along such fibers carry data, telephone signals, and television programs—all at once, if required. They use low-powered semiconductor diode lasers, which can also be made small enough to fit inside a portable compact disk player.

A laser beam travels in a straight line, which makes it useful in leveling instruments used in the construction industry. Alongside the Bosporus Bridge in Turkey and across the San Andreas Fault in California—both active earthquake areas—there are permanent laser beams aimed at a detector to give advance warning of the slightest earth movements.

Lasers can also be used to produce holograms, for storing 3-D graphics, and for detecting credit card forgeries.

Hologram
A 3-D image of an object or scene, created using laser light. Some holograms must be viewed in laser light; others can be viewed in normal light.

Invisible Radiations

Light is one type of electromagnetic radiation. Beyond the visible spectrum, extending to both longer and shorter wavelengths, are other types of electromagnetic radiation. They range from long-wavelength radio waves to ultra-short-wavelength gamma rays.

Curriculum Context

For many curricula, students should know that radio waves, light, and X-rays are different wavelength bands in the spectrum of electromagnetic waves.

Ultraviolet and infrared

Just beyond the visible spectrum, at shorter wavelengths than those of visible light, lies ultraviolet radiation. It is invisible to human eyes, but can be seen by birds and some insects. At longer wavelengths, on the other side of the visible spectrum, lies infrared radiation. It can be detected by animals such as pit vipers. Infrared radiation is given off by anything hotter than its surroundings. The Sun produces both kinds of radiation as well as visible light.

X rays and gamma rays

The electromagnetic spectrum extends beyond the ultraviolet and the infrared. Shorter wavelengths, in the range 1 to 10^{-6} nanometers, consist of X rays and gamma rays. X rays are produced by changes in metal atoms that have been made unstable by being bombarded by a stream of electrons. In an X-ray tube, a cathode consisting of a wire filament is heated red-hot by an extremely high-voltage electric current (up to 2 million volts). The anode consists of a lump of copper, which often has water pipes incorporated in it to keep it cool. Attached to the copper is a slice of the heavy metal tungsten, termed the target.

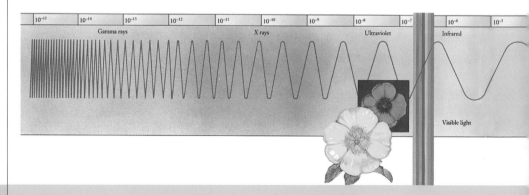

| 10^{-15} | 10^{-14} | 10^{-13} | 10^{-12} | 10^{-11} | 10^{-10} | 10^{-9} | 10^{-8} | 10^{-7} | 10^{-6} | 10^{-5} |

Gamma rays · X rays · Ultraviolet · Infrared · Visible light

This image of the Crab Nebula combines data from different parts of the electromagnetic spectrum. The light blue is an X-ray image from the Chandra space telescope; the yellow is an optical image from the Hubble space telescope; and the red is an infrared image from the Spitzer space telescope.

Electrons boil off the cathode and stream toward the target, where they excite tungsten atoms, in which electron "jumps" result in the emission of X rays. The rays, emitted at right angles to the electron beam, pass through a window in the side of the X-ray tube. The energy of the X rays depends on the voltage applied to the tube. Their chief use is in medicine, but they are also used in analytical science.

X rays do not occur naturally on Earth, although they are emitted by certain stars and other celestial bodies. So, too, are gamma rays, which are even more energetic than X rays. They do occur on Earth as an accompaniment to the decay of various radioactive elements, such as isotopes of radium and uranium. Unlike X rays, which arise from excitation of electrons in an atom, they are produced by changes that take place in an atom's nucleus. They are used to take "X-ray" photographs of metallic objects, and to sterilize food and medical equipment.

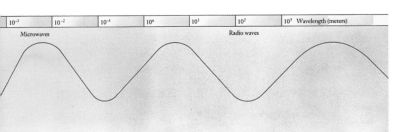

The electromagnetic spectrum. Gamma rays have the shortest wavelength and highest radiation; radio waves the longest wavelength and lowest energy.

Radio Waves

The long-wavelength end of the electromagnetic spectrum is occupied by radio waves. They range from microwaves, with wavelengths of tiny fractions of an inch to 12 inches (0.1 to 30 cm), to radio waves with wavelengths of several hundred yards (meters).

Microwaves

At the shorter end of the radio spectrum, microwaves are used for satellite communications, in radar, for cooking food, and also for direct local radio communications. For longer distance communications on Earth, microwave signals must be relayed between tall towers that are located up to 50 kilometers (30 miles) apart, the line-of-sight distance.

Microwaves are generated in special electron tubes (valves), in which a high-frequency electric field varies the speeds of streams of electrons. This makes them resonate in a metal cavity, producing microwaves. A typical microwave-transmitting valve, called a klystron, is made of metal and works at very high voltages. The waves are transmitted and received by dish-shaped antennas, which focus a beam of microwaves as a curved mirror focuses a beam of light.

Quasar

(quasi-stellar radio source) A type of very distant galaxy that may be invisible in the visible spectrum but is a powerful source of radio emissions. Quasars have a powerfully energetic galactic nucleus.

Exploding galaxies called quasars and distant clouds of interstellar gas emit microwaves, which are detected by large radio telescopes. Like other forms of electromagnetic radiation, the waves travel through space at the speed of light. Using computers to analyze microwave signals picked up by radio telescopes, astronomers can construct radio maps of celestial objects such as galaxies.

Radio waves

Electromagnetic radiation of wavelengths greater than 30 cm are usually known simply as radio waves. They are also produced by oscillating electrons in wires or

Frequency Modulation and Amplitude Modulation

Radio broadcasts use two kinds of signal modulation. In frequency modulation (FM), the broadcast signal varies the frequency of the carrier wave. In amplitude modulation (AM), the amplitude is varied. FM transmissions use short wavelengths. Like microwaves, their range is limited to line of sight, but the quality of reception is normally good. AM transmissions may use extremely long wavelengths. They can bounce off layers of ionized gas in the atmosphere and so travel long distances. However, the quality of reception is generally poorer than that of FM.

transmitting valves, and are used mostly for communications. The actual transmitter consists of a metal wire or rod, which sends radio waves into the air.

Special techniques make the transmitted wave carry data or signals corresponding to speech, music, or pictures. The transmitter emits a continuous radio wave, at a particular wavelength, called a carrier wave. Like any other wave, it has a characteristic frequency (number of waves per second) and amplitude (wave height). The signal to be broadcast is made to vary, or modulate, the carrier wave. At the receiver, the broadcast signal is picked up by an antenna and then demodulated—the carrier wave is removed, leaving the audio-frequency signal.

Early radio telescopes had dishes as large as possible, to collect radio waves over the maximum area. Today, computers can combine the signals received from arrays of smaller telescopes, which together act like a giant telescope with a dish several miles (km) wide.

Radar

Long-range radio communications depend on the reflection of radio waves off the ionosphere (one of the upper layers of the atmosphere). In the late 1930s, scientists in Britain and Germany independently discovered that large solid objects, such as ships and aircraft, also reflect radio waves in the microwave region. The system was developed initially for the military and became known as RAdio Detection And Ranging, or radar.

Ionosphere

Layers of ionized (charged) gases in the Earth's upper atmosphere.

Antenna

A device for transmitting and receiving radio signals. Antennas can take many forms, ranging from a single piece of wire to a sophisticated parabolic dish.

A typical radar system

In a typical radar system, an antenna transmits microwave signals of wavelength 1–10 cm. The signals travel at the speed of light (300,000 kilometers, or 186,000 miles, per second) to the target, which reflects part of them back to a receiving antenna—which is the same as the transmitting antenna. The echoes are displayed, usually on a television-type screen called a plan position indicator (PPI).

Some transmitting antennas consist of a metal mesh dish or array that can be aimed toward the target. In others, the antenna rotates to make the radar signal search a wide area. In most modern radar devices, this rotation is achieved electronically, and the antenna itself does not move. Because there is only a single antenna, each type of radar has a switching device to make it alternate rapidly between transmitting and receiving.

Doppler radar

Most radar systems concentrate the transmitted signals into parallel beams of pulses, rather than continuous waves, and the range of a target is found by measuring the time taken for a pulse to be reflected back. The frequency of the returning signal can also provide information. If the target is moving, there is a change in the frequency of the echo caused by the Doppler effect (see pages 66–67). If the target is approaching, for example, the reflected microwaves have a higher frequency than the original signal. For a receding target, the frequency of the reflected wave is lower. From the magnitude of the frequency change, the speed of the approaching target can be calculated.

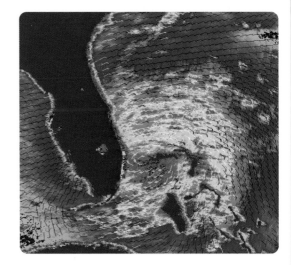

Doppler radars are used by the police to measure the speeds of road vehicles. The Doppler effect also allows continuous-wave radar systems to ignore stationary objects and display only targets that are moving. This suppresses echoes of buildings and hills, preventing clutter on the radar display.

Astronomers use Doppler radars mounted on satellites to determine the direction and speed of rotation of planets. This is done by pointing the radar at the equatorial edge of a planet to measure its speed of approach or departure. Meteorologists also use satellite radar to plot weather systems—particularly the density of rain clouds—for compiling weather maps and forecasts. Other satellite-borne radar systems accurately measure the heights of mountains on land and under the oceans to construct radar maps of the Earth's surface. Similar radars have even been used to penetrate the dense clouds in the atmosphere of Venus and produce maps of the planet's surface.

In 2005 Hurricane Katrina caused devastation around New Orleans, Louisiana. This image shows Katrina while it was still a tropical storm, off the coast of Florida. The data for the image was gathered using a special kind of radar called a scatterometer. This type of instrument gives accurate measurements of wind speed and direction.

Subatomic Particles

Many physical phenomena can be explained in terms of the behavior of atoms. Most optical and electrical effects, for example, involve the production or movement of electrons—negatively charged subatomic particles in orbit around a central, positively charged nucleus.

Subatomic particles

The principal subatomic particles—components of an atom—are the electron, proton, and neutron. Protons and neutrons are normally located in an atom's nucleus, which is surrounded by orbiting electrons. A simple model of the atom gradually emerged in the early years of the 20th century as the various particles were discovered.

The electron was discovered by the British physicist Joseph Thomson (1856–1940) in 1897. He studied cathode rays, emitted by the cathode (negative electrode) of a vacuum tube. Thomson showed that the "rays" actually consist of tiny charged particles, which he called electrons. The term "cathode ray" persists in the name of the cathode-ray tube, used in older television sets, radar displays, and computer terminals. All of these devices utilize a beam of electrons (from a cathode) in order to excite the light-emitting phosphors on the inside of the tube's screen.

The nucleus

The existence of the tiny atomic nucleus was deduced from experiments carried out by the New Zealand-born physicist Ernest Rutherford (1871–1937) in 1911. He demonstrated that the nucleus has a positive charge, and later discovered that the charge carrier is the proton (whose charge is equal but opposite to that of an electron). Rutherford also showed that a proton is very much more massive than an electron. Protons are

This image shows the meeting of a particle called a neutrino with an electron (arrow) in a bubble chamber. Bubble chambers "magnify" the tracks of subatomic particles, making it possible to record snapshots of their movements. They have largely been replaced by more sophisticated detectors, but no other kind of detector shows such a direct record of a particle's movement.

about 1800 times as massive as electrons. The number of protons in an atom's nucleus equals the number of orbiting electrons, so that the atom has no overall electric charge.

Neutrons

Every element has a different number of protons, and it is this number—the atomic number—that gives a particular element its identity. But the protons alone do not account for the total mass of a nucleus (except in the case of hydrogen). The remainder of the nuclear mass comes from neutrons, the other major subatomic particles, discovered in 1932 by the British physicist James Chadwick (1891–1974). A neutron carries no electric charge, and has a mass almost exactly the same as that of a proton.

Hadrons and leptons

Later discoveries made this simple model of the atom —protons and neutrons in the nucleus, surrounded by electrons in orbit—obsolete. In addition to protons,

Quarks

An even smaller subatomic particle, called the quark, was proposed in 1962 by the United States physicist Murray Gell-Mann to clarify the confusion caused by the incomplete identification of subatomic particles. The quark is a hypothetical fundamental particle devised to explain the existence and behavior of all the other kinds of particle. At least 12 different kinds of quark (and antiquark) have now been described. They combine to form protons, neutrons, and various other subatomic—but no longer fundamental—particles. Quarks have fractional electric charges of either $+^2/_3$ or $-^1/_3$. A proton consists of three quarks of charges $^2/_3$, $^2/_3$, and $-^1/_3$, giving an overall charge of +1. A neutron also consists of three quarks, which have charges of $^2/_3$, $-^1/_3$, and $-^1/_3$. This results in an overall charge of zero. Pi mesons consist of only two quarks.

Curriculum Context

For many curricula, students should know that protons and neutrons have substructures and consist of particles called quarks.

neutrons, and electrons, other subatomic particles began to turn up, often after their existence had been predicted to account for the behavior of atoms and other particles. These included the pi meson (with mass between that of a proton and an electron) and the positron (a positively-charged particle with mass equal to that of an electron).

Since the development in the 1930s of particle accelerators such as the cyclotron, collectively nicknamed "atom smashers," more than 30 other particles have been identified, although their role in atomic—usually nuclear—structure was not always clear. They are classified into two main types: those with no apparent internal structure, such as the electron, positron, muon, neutrino, and tau particle, are collectively called leptons. The second group—the proton, neutron, and pi meson—are called hadrons, which do have an internal structure.

The Unstable Atom

An element's chemical identity is determined by the number of protons in the nuclei of its atoms. Elements are listed in the Periodic Table in order of the number of protons in the nucleus—their atomic number. Hydrogen has 1 proton, helium 2, lithium 3, beryllium 4, and so on right through to the heaviest naturally occurring element, uranium, with 92 protons.

The number of neutrons in the atomic nuclei also increases along the list, but in a less predictable way. Helium has 2 neutrons, lithium 3, beryllium 5, and uranium as many as 146. Uranium and some other elements have two or more forms with different numbers of neutrons in their nuclei. These forms, called isotopes, have the same numbers of protons (and hence the same chemical identity), but the differing number of neutrons gives them different masses. Uranium, for example, has isotopes of masses 234, 235, and 238.

Radioactive decay

Some combinations of protons and neutrons are unstable because of forces acting within their nuclei. They spontaneously disintegrate, usually by emitting an alpha particle (two protons and two neutrons) or a beta particle (an electron). Penetrating gamma rays may be emitted at the same time, and the whole phenomenon is called radioactivity. Because an alpha emitter loses two protons and two neutrons, it turns into a different element whose atomic number is therefore two less. Radium-226 (the isotope of radium with mass 226), of atomic number 88, decays by emitting alpha particles to become the gaseous element radon, atomic number 86, mass 222.

In the nucleus of a beta-emitting radioactive isotope, a neutron changes into a proton and releases an electron (beta particle). This results in no significant change in

Curriculum Context

For many curricula, students should understand that each element has a specific number of protons in the nucleus, and each isotope of the element has a different but specific number of neutrons in the nucleus.

Curriculum Context

For many curricula, students should understand the three most common forms of radioactive decay (alpha, beta, and gamma) and know how the nucleus changes in each type of decay.

mass but an increase of one in atomic number, with again the formation of a different element. For example, radium-228 (atomic number 88) emits beta particles to become actinium-228 (atomic number 89). In both of these examples, radioactive decay takes the form of a cascade, resulting in products that are themselves radioactive, and go on to form yet other elements—which in turn experience radioactive decay. Uranium-238 decays by emitting both alpha and beta particles, passing through 14 different stages before eventually finishing as the stable element lead-206.

Radioactive half-life

Not all radioactive isotopes decay at the same rate; nor do all the atoms in a sample disintegrate simultaneously. Physicists express the rate in terms of an element's half-life—the time it takes for half the atoms to decay into other atoms. The naturally occurring element thorium-232 has a half-life of nearly 14 billion years; some isotopes, created in cyclotrons, have half-lives of only a few hundred thousandths of a second.

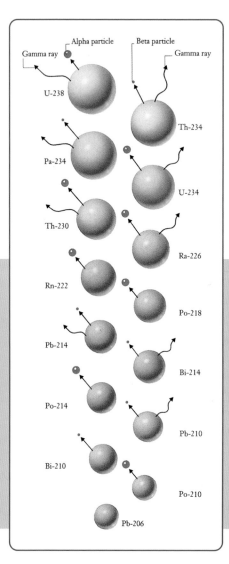

Gamma ray
Alpha particle
Beta particle
Gamma ray
U-238
Th-234
Pa-234
U-234
Th-230
Ra-226
Rn-222
Po-218
Pb-214
Bi-214
Po-214
Pb-210
Bi-210
Po-210
Pb-206

Natural Decay

There are three natural radioactive decay series, beginning with the isotopes thorium-232, uranium-235, and uranium-238 (shown here). This series involves a chain of 14 different radioactive isotopes—of thorium (Th), protactinium (Pa), radium (Ra), radon (Rn), polonium (Po), lead (Pb), and bismuth (Bi)—before ending with the nonradioactive lead-206. Each isotope in the chain emits alpha particles, beta particles, gamma rays, or a combination.

By looking at which rock layers fossils occur in, scientists can work out their relative age. They could say, for example, that these trilobites lived long before the first dinosaurs. However, radiometric dating is needed to discover their absolute age. Trilobites flourished during the Cambrian period, 543 to 490 million years ago.

Radiometric dating

Identifying a radioactive isotope in an object, and knowing its half-life, provides a way of estimating the object's age. Anything made of wood, for example, contains tiny amounts of radioactive carbon-14, absorbed from the atmosphere while the tree was alive. After the tree dies, the wood no longer absorbs carbon-14, and so the proportion of this isotope in the wood gradually falls as the carbon-14 decays. In radiocarbon dating, the amount of carbon-14 is measured and the age of the wood calculated from the knowledge that carbon-14's half-life is 5770 years (it decays to form ordinary nitrogen-14). Radiocarbon dating can also be used to estimate the age of anything that was once a living organism.

Beyond about 60,000 years the levels of carbon-14 fall so low that the technique is no longer accurate. However, similar radio-dating methods, using isotopes with much longer half-lives, are used to determine the ages of rocks. Potassium–argon dating, for example, is used to date very ancient rocks. Potassium-40 is a naturally occurring radioactive isotope that decays to argon-40 with a half-life of 1.3 billion years.

Nuclear Fission

Slow spontaneous disintegration in the nuclei of their atoms makes radioactive elements unstable. Bombarding the nuclei with neutrons speeds up the disintegration or makes a stable nucleus unstable. The nuclei absorb the neutrons and split, releasing energy. This is because the mass of the fission products is fractionally less than the mass of the split nucleus. This "lost" mass is converted into energy.

Nuclear energy

With some atoms, splitting the nucleus (fission) sometimes produces more neutrons. If these in turn are absorbed by other nuclei, which then split, producing even more neutrons, a rapidly accelerating process called a chain reaction may result. Uncontrolled, it results in a nuclear explosion. A controlled reaction forms the basis of a reaction that can be harnessed as nuclear energy.

One of the first materials used in controlled fission—in a nuclear reactor—was the isotope uranium-235. It occurs as a very small percentage (0.72 percent) of natural uranium, which consists mainly of stable uranium-238. When removed from natural uranium, uranium-235 can be used as a nuclear fuel.

Controlling the reaction

Fission is more likely to occur if the bombarding neutrons are moving slowly. The uranium fuel in a reactor is surrounded by a moderator such as graphite or heavy water—deuterium oxide (D_2O). The reactor also has control rods, which can be moved into or out of the reactor core to speed up or slow down the chain reaction. The control rods are made from the elements boron and cadmium, which absorb neutrons without undergoing fission. They act as "sponges", mopping up stray neutrons and damping down the reaction.

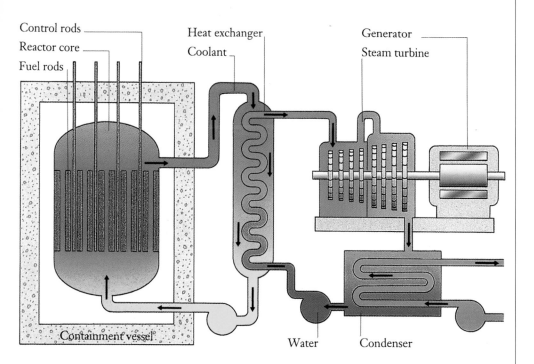

Control rods
Reactor core
Fuel rods
Heat exchanger
Coolant
Generator
Steam turbine
Containment vessel
Water
Condenser

Cooling

The intense heat produced inside the reactor's core is absorbed by a fluid and carried to an external heat exchanger. The fluid becomes highly radioactive and is recycled around a closed system within the reactor. Most reactors use water as a coolant kept under pressure to let it reach a high temperature without boiling (a pressurized-water reactor). An advanced gas-cooled reactor uses carbon dioxide gas instead of water. The heat carried away to the heat exchanger is used to boil water for making steam, which drives turbines for generating electricity.

A design using enriched uranium or plutonium-239 as fuel is called a fast reactor because no moderator is employed. The core gets so hot that liquid sodium metal has to be used as a coolant.

At a nuclear power plant, the reactor is merely a type of boiler for heating water to make steam. A gas or liquid coolant flowing through the hot reactor core passes beyond the heavily shielded containment vessel to enter a heat exchanger. There it boils water and the steam passes to steam turbines connected to an electricity generator.

Nuclear Fusion

Fusion is a nuclear reaction in which the nuclei of light atoms combine to form heavier, more stable nuclei. It takes place in the Sun and other stars, which "burn" hydrogen in their cores. If scientists can copy the fusion reaction, it could become a clean and safe source of energy for the future.

Deuterium
An isotope of hydrogen with a mass of two—one proton, one neutron.

Tritium
Another isotope of hydrogen with a mass of three—one proton and two neutrons.

The fusion reaction
In the fusion reaction, two hydrogen nuclei (protons) combine to form deuterium. Further fusion of the deuterium results in the formation of helium, with the release of vast amounts of heat and light. As in nuclear fission, the mass of the products is slightly less than those of the reactants, and the missing mass appears as energy. However, unlike fission, the products of fusion are not radioactive.

Scientists who were trying to copy this reaction on Earth discovered that the best starting materials are deuterium and tritium. In this fusion reaction, an atom of deuterium combines with an atom of tritium to form an atom of helium, with the release of a neutron and vast amounts of heat energy.

Because both deuterium and tritium nuclei have a positive electric charge, they are reluctant to fuse except at extremely high temperatures (about 100 million degrees K). Such temperatures were first achieved artificially in a hydrogen bomb, in which the fusion reaction is allowed to go out of control.

Fusion reactors
Today scientists are trying to produce controlled fusion. The chief difficulty is that, at such high temperatures, the combining gases exist as the fourth state of matter known as a plasma. The negative electrons and positive hydrogen nuclei are separated to give a completely

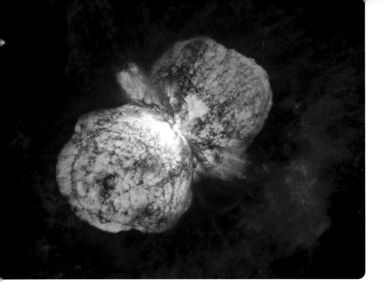

Massive stars burn through their fuel more quickly than the Sun. When hydrogen fuel runs out, the core of the star heats up, and further fusion reactions form heavier elements. Eventually, iron forms at the core, and cannot fuse any further. The core collapses, then internal forces blast it open in a massive explosion—a supernova. The star Eta Carinae, shown here, is near the end of its life. A small explosion in 1840 pushed out the vast gas clouds that now surround the star. But the final supernova will be many times more powerful.

ionized fluid, which can be contained only by powerful magnetic fields—no physical container could withstand the extremely high temperatures produced in a fusion reaction.

Attempted solutions to the fusion problem usually involve containing the plasma in a magnetic "bottle," which may be shaped like a figure of eight or like a doughnut (called a torus). The Tokamak reactor consists of a torus surrounded by D-shaped coils. Pulses of high-voltage current in the coils create the plasma and raise its temperature.

Despite many years of research, a sustained, controlled fusion reaction has yet to be demonstrated. It could be many more years before fusion can be used as a clean energy source.

Laser Fusion

Fusion using lasers is an alternative method to using a tokamak. One kind of laser fusion uses a long magnetic "bottle." Tiny glass pellets containing deuterium and tritium gas are introduced into the bottle and bombarded by flashes of laser light. This vaporizes the glass and raises the gases to the plasma state and fusion temperature.

Waves and Particles

Electrons were discovered first in cathode rays, which are streams of particles given off by a cathode in a vacuum tube (as in a cathode-ray tube). Physicists soon determined the mass of the electron, and found it to be about 0.0005 of that of a hydrogen atom. Today they use sophisticated equipment to accelerate electrons to very high speeds and use them as "bullets" to smash atoms in cyclotrons.

Cyclotron

A type of particle accelerator that uses high-energy electric and magnetic fields to accelerate charged particles along a circular path, so that they re-encounter the accelerating fields many times.

Electrons as waves

Light waves can be considered as made up of particles (photons). If a light wave can be made up of particles, could electrons—which are usually regarded as tiny particles—behave like a wave? This question was first asked by the French physicist Louis de Broglie, who in 1924 proposed that the answer is yes.

One phenomenon of light that demonstrates its wave nature is interference—the alternate reinforcement and cancellation that take place when two similar waves come together, creating light and dark bands or rings. A few years after de Broglie's prediction, scientists in the United States and Britain produced interference patterns by scattering electrons from the surface of a metal crystal or in thin metal foil. They had demonstrated the existence of electron waves.

Another well-known property of light is that it can be focused by lenses to make optical instruments such as telescopes and microscopes. Because electrons carry a (negative) electric charge, a circular electromagnet around an electron beam can be used to focus it just as a lens focuses light. A series of magnetic lenses are employed in this way in an electron microscope, which utilizes the very short wavelength of electron waves to produce images of objects that are far too small to be seen even with the most powerful optical microscopes.

The wavelength of the bands of light in an element's spectrum—produced, for example, when it is heated to incandescence—correspond to the energies of the photons released when its atoms' electrons "jump" between permissible energy levels. If electrons absorb energy, they become excited and move to higher energy levels. Then, as they return to their normal level (their ground state), they part with their extra energy as photons.

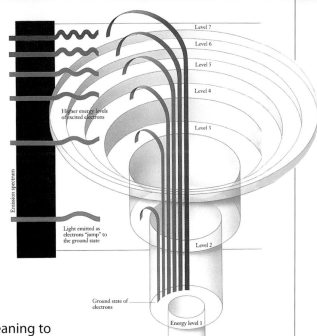

Emission spectrum

Higher energy levels of excited electrons

Light emitted as electrons "jump" to the ground state

Level 7
Level 6
Level 5
Level 4
Level 3
Level 2

Ground state of electrons

Energy level 1

Nucleus

Electron orbitals

These discoveries gave new meaning to quantum theory (see page 102). The probability of locating an electron in an atom turns out to be a wave function that describes the state of an electron in a given orbital, including such factors as its spin, angular momentum, and likely position in space. For example, an atom's innermost—lowest energy—electrons have zero angular momentum and are located in a spherical orbital centered on the nucleus. The electrons in the next highest energy level have an angular momentum of 1 and occupy three dumbbell-shaped orbitals at right angles to each other. Waves are equated with probabilities, which in turn specify shapes.

Using this combined theory, called wave mechanics, it is now possible to explain all the phenomena of physics. In particular, the characteristic light emitted by a particular element—its spectral "fingerprint"—corresponds to a wave, or photons, emitted as electrons change orbitals after absorbing energy. This explanation was first offered as long ago as the year 1900 by the German physicist Max Planck when he first proposed quantum theory, which was to have such a dramatic effect on 20th-century physics.

Curriculum Context

For many curricula, students should understand that spectral lines are the result of transitions of electrons between energy levels and that these lines correspond to photons with a frequency related to the energy spacing between levels.

Quantum Physics

When atoms emit electromagnetic radiation—as when atoms of a metal heated to the point of incandescence give off light—the radiation has a characteristic wavelength rather than a continuous range of energies. Light is emitted when electrons "jump" between an orbit of high energy to one at a lower energy level.

Each jump releases a "packet" of light energy, called a quantum, equal to the difference in energies between the two atomic orbits. Light quanta are known as photons, and in many respects they can be regarded as particles with a mass of zero but a specific amount of energy and momentum.

Particle theory of light

The particle theory of light has potential practical applications. One proposal for powering future interstellar spacecraft uses huge sails to gather sunlight. The millions of photons hitting the sails would push the craft along. The principle is easy to understand in terms of particle-like photons; it is more difficult if light is thought of as electromagnetic waves.

Another phenomenon that could not be explained in terms of the wave theory of light is the photoelectric effect. This is the release of electrons from the surface of a material (usually a metal) when it is struck by light, X rays or gamma rays. Atoms in the material absorb photons from the incident radiation. The photons transfer sufficient energy to some electrons to enable them to escape.

Many other physical phenomena described in terms of waves of energy can also be explained by quantum theory. But there is no one "correct" theory: waves or quanta can be chosen, whichever is convenient for the purposes of explanation.

Electron orbitals

Electrons in an atom are often shown orbiting the nucleus in fixed circular orbits like planets orbiting the Sun. A better model, developed alongside quantum theory, visualizes electrons as occupying regions in space, and there is a definite probability that a particular electron will be in a certain place at a certain time. The region in which the electron is likely to be found is called an orbital.

Probability—not certainty—is involved because of a principle put forward by the German physicist Werner Heisenberg in 1927. Heisenberg argued that it is not possible to know simultaneously the precise position and momentum of an electron. Probability is a mathematical concept, and modern physicists and chemists deal with electrons using equations whose terms are probability functions. This approach is known as quantum mechanics.

Other quanta

Physicists now deal with many other kinds of quanta, as well as photons. For example, the thermal vibrations of atoms in the lattice of a crystal correspond to discrete energy states whose quantum is the phonon. A roton is a quantum of rotational energy, and a magnon is the quantum of spin energy of the molecular magnets in a magnetic substance.

Electrons in an atom and the nuclei themselves also spin, and this spin is quantized (and ascribed a quantum number). Transitions or "jumps" between the two possible spin states of the outer electron in a cesium atom are exploited in the cesium clock, which is accurate to within a second in 20 million years.

Curriculum Context

For many curricula, students should understand that at subatomic scales, the wavelike nature of matter becomes important, and quantum mechanics better describes the behavior of subatomic particles than Newtonian mechanics.

Mass Equals Energy

Large amounts of energy—mostly heat—are produced by nuclear fission or fusion because the masses of the products of the reaction are slightly less than the masses of the reactants. This "lost" mass—the difference between the two—appears as energy. The interchangeability of mass and energy was predicted in 1905 by the German-born physicist Albert Einstein in his special theory of relativity.

Constant speed of light

A key principle behind Einstein's special theory of relativity is that the speed of light in a vacuum is constant, even if the source of light is moving in relation to an observer. For example, if light is projected from an aircraft in flight, the light moves forward at a constant speed no matter how fast the plane is flying. The speed of light in a vacuum is about 186,000 miles per second (300,000 km/sec), and is represented by the letter c.

Strange effects occur when something moves at very high speeds. To a stationary observer, a hypothetical spacecraft traveling at half the speed of light appears to get shorter (by about 13 percent) and more massive (by the same proportion). The relative increase in mass equals the energy given to the spacecraft to accelerate it. Einstein showed that any mass has an energy equivalent, and that the energy is equal to the mass multiplied by the square of the speed of light. In mathematical terms, this is expressed by the equation:

$$E = mc^2.$$

Einstein adopted the accepted principle that light travels by the shortest distance between two points. But when he proposed that time is the fourth dimension, he found that massive objects in space, such as stars and galaxies, distort spacetime through

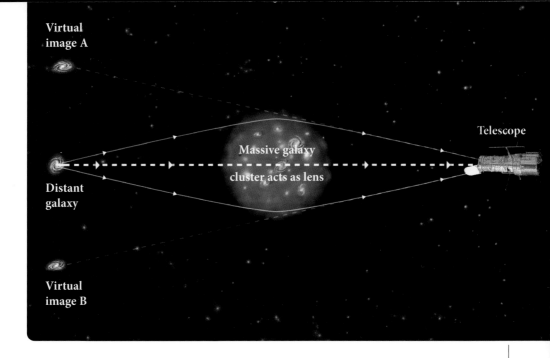

Virtual
image A

Telescope

Massive galaxy
cluster acts as lens

Distant
galaxy

Virtual
image B

gravitational effects. And where spacetime is curved,
light follows a curved—though still the shortest—path.

General relativity

This behavior of light is a consequence of Einstein's
general theory of relativity (1916). It has since been
verified by various astronomical observations. In one
of these, the path of light from a distant star is seen to
be curved when it passes close to the Sun. More
recently, radio astronomers have captured images of
what appear to be a pair of quasars (very distant, very
bright stars), located at the same distance from Earth.
There is only one quasar, but radiation from it passes
close to an intervening galaxy. The galaxy acts as a
gravitational lens, bending the radiation so that, from
Earth, it appears to originate in a different place from
the radiation that travels directly to Earth.

Einstein also tried to combine his relativity theory with
the quantum theory. This ideal, the unified field theory,
still occupies many physicists, although others believe
that it will never be achieved.

Gravitational lensing.
A cluster of galaxies
that lies between a
distant galaxy and a
telescope is so
massive that it makes
spacetime curve.
Light rays from the
distant galaxy follow
this curved path, so
that the telescope
sees two images of a
galaxy that should be
invisible from Earth.

Glossary

Allotropes Forms of an element with different physical properties. A good example is the element carbon, which occurs naturally as graphite, diamond, and amorphous carbon.

Amorphous Having no regular structure.

Ammeter An instrument for measuring the flow of electric current in a circuit.

Anion A negative ion.

Anode A positive electrode.

Anodizing A method of electroplating an object in which the object to be plated is placed at the anode rather than the cathode.

Antenna A device for transmitting and receiving radio signals. Antennas can take many forms, ranging from a single piece of wire to a sophisticated parabolic dish.

Armature The central, rotating part of an electric motor, usually consisting of several wire coils wound at different angles.

Cathode A negative electrode.

Cation A positive ion.

Ceramic A strong, brittle, nonmetallic material made by heating the raw materials to high temperatures.

Combined-cycle power station A power station in which exhaust gas from a gas turbine heats water to produce steam to power a steam turbine. The combination of gas and steam turbines allows a more efficient use of fuel.

Commutator A segmented, sliding contact that acts to rapidly reverse the direction of current flow into an electric motor.

Cryogenics Study of the physics of materials at very low temperatures.

Cyclotron A type of particle accelerator that uses high-energy electric and magnetic fields to accelerate charged particles along a circular path, so that they re-encounter the accelerating fields many times.

Deuterium An isotope of hydrogen with a mass of two—one proton and one neutron.

Doping Adding small amounts of another substance to a pure sample of an element in order to change its properties.

Electrochemical cell A device that generates an electric voltage from chemical reactions. A battery is a combination of two or more electrochemical cells.

Electrode A conductor used as the positive or negative terminal through which electric current passes between metallic and nonmetallic parts of an electric circuit.

Electromagnetic induction The process by which a changing magnetic field creates an electric field, or a changing electric field produces a magnetic field.

Entropy A measure of the amount of disorder in a system.

Free fall The ideal falling motion of an object subject only to the force of gravity. The acceleration of an object in free fall is approx. 30 feet/sec^2 (9 m/sec^2).

Heat engine An engine such as an internal combustion engine, steam engine, or steam turbine, in which a fuel is burned to produce heat, which is then used in some way to do useful work.

Hertz (Hz) The unit of frequency. 1 Hz = 1 cycle per second.

Hologram A 3-D image of an object or scene, created using laser light. Some holograms must be viewed in laser light; others can be viewed in normal light.

Hydraulics Mechanisms that use the pressure caused by a relatively small force on a small piston to produce a very large force on a larger piston.

Incandescent The emission of light by a hot body. The color of light emitted is related to temperature.

Inertia The tendency of an object to continue in its state of rest or uniform motion unless acted upon by an external force. The greater the mass of an object, the greater its inertia.

Insulator A nonmetallic element or compound that resists the flow of electricity through it.

Ionosphere Layers of ionized (charged) gases in the Earth's upper atmosphere.

Isotopes Forms of an element with the same numbers of protons in the nucleus but different numbers of neutrons.

Kilocalorie 1 kilocalorie = the amount of heat needed to raise the temperature of a kilogram of water through 1 degree Celsius.

Kinetic energy The energy of movement.

Magnetic field The region around a magnet in which its magnetic forces act.

Mole The molecular mass of a substance expressed in grams.

MRI scanner MRI stands for magnetic resonance imaging. MRI scanners can produce images of the organs inside the body. They are used in medical diagnosis. Unlike X rays they show soft tissue better than bones.

Normal The normal is a line at right angles to a plane or surface.

Plasma A fourth state of matter, which exists at very high temperatures. In plasma, matter has so much energy that the atoms break up into electrically charged fragments.

Potential energy Stored energy. In gravitational potential energy the energy is due to position. Potential energy can also be stored in a spring or other elastic object.

Pressure cooker A kitchen appliance used widely in the past to cook food more quickly. Today it has been largely superseded by the microwave.

Sine The sine of an angle in a right-angled triangle is the ratio of the length of the opposite side to the length of the hypotenuse (the longest side).

Spectrum A range of electromagnetic wavelengths (or frequencies), in order of increasing or decreasing wavelength. The spectrum of light covers only visible wavelengths, from red to violet.

Standing wave A stationary pattern of waves produced by two waves of the same frequency traveling in opposite directions.

Stator The outer, stationary part of an electric motor. This may consist of a permanent magnet or a series of electromagnetic coils.

Supersonic Faster than the speed of sound.

Tensile strength The ability of a material to resist longitudinal force (tension)—the force required to pull it apart.

Thermodynamics The scientific study of how heat is transferred between objects, the ways in which other forms of energy are converted into heat, and the ways in which heat can be converted to other forms of energy.

Transformer A device in which alternating current of one voltage can be raised or lowered to another voltage.

Tritium Another isotope of hydrogen with a mass of three—one proton and two neutrons.

Worm gear A rod with a screw thread (the worm) that meshes with a toothed wheel (the worm wheel). It is used to convert rotary motion in one shaft to rotary motion in another shaft at right angles to the first. It can also change the speed and power of the rotation.

Further Research

BOOKS

Atkins, Peter. *Four Laws That Drive the Universe*. Oxford: Oxford University Press, 2007.

Bloomfield, Louis. *How Things Work: The Physics of Everyday Life.* Hoboken: Wiley, 2009.

Cropper, William H. *Great Physicists: The Life and Times of Leading Physicists from Galileo to Hawking.* New York: OUP USA, 2004.

Feynman, Richard. *Six Easy Pieces: Fundamentals of Physics Explained.* London: Penguin, 2007.

Feynman, Richard. *Six Not-so-easy Pieces: Einstein's Relativity, Symmetry and Space-time.* London: Penguin, 2007.

Gamow, George. *Thirty Years That Shook Physics: The Story of Quantum Theory*. Mineola: Dover, 1986.

Gonick, Larry and Art Huffman. *The Cartoon Guide to Physics.* London: HarperCollins, 1991.

Kirkland, Kyle. *Physics in Our World: Electricity and Magnetism.* New York: Facts on File, 2007.

Morris, Neil. *Energy Now and In the Future: The Energy Mix: Now and in the Future.* London: Franklin Watts, 2009.

Morus, Iwan Rhys. *Michael Faraday and the Electrical Century*. London: Icon Books, 2004.

Pople, Stephen and Charles Taylor. *Science.* Oxford: Oxford University Press, 2004.

Rhodes, Richard, *The Making of the Atomic Bomb.* New York: Simon & Shuster, 1986.

Smith, Alastair. *Forces, Energy and Motion*. London: Usborne, 2001.

Solway, Andrew. *The Physical Sciences: Electricity and Magnetism*. London: Wayland, 2007.

Solway, Andrew. *The Physical Sciences: Energy*. London: Wayland, 2007.

DVD

NOVA: *Physics—The Elegant Universe and Beyond*. PBS, 2003.

INTERNET RESOURCES

How Things Work Student Companion Site. An online site with additional resources to go with Louis Bloomfield's book on the physics of everyday life.
http://bcs.wiley.com/he-bcs/Books?action=index&itemId=047146886X&bcsId=2880

Hyperphysics. Comprehensive coverage of the subject on an award-winning website created by Georgia State University.
http://hyperphysics.phy-astr.gsu.edu/hbase/hframe.html

New Scientist. The latest news and limited access to articles from *New Scientist* magazine. http://www.newscientist.com/

Science Museum: Physics and Maths. Interesting features on many aspects of physics, including accurate measurement, atomic clocks, and nuclear power.
http://www.sciencemuseum.org.uk/onlinestuff/subjects/physics_and_maths.aspx

Scientific American. Breaking news and some access to features and articles from *Scientific American* magazine.
http://www.sciam.com/

The Naked Scientists. A website covering all aspects of science, including physics, based on a series of radio programs created by a group of Cambridge University physicians and researchers.
http://www.thenakedscientists.com

The National Renewable Energy Laboratory (NREL). This website includes overviews of different kinds of alternative energy and information on research in these areas at NREL.
http://www.nrel.gov/

The Nobel Prize in Physics. The Nobel Prize website includes biographical information on the many eminent physicists who have won this ultimate science prize.
http://nobelprize.org/nobel_prizes/physics/

The Physics Classroom. Clear and easy to understand coverage of high-school level physics, originally developed for Glenbrook South High School in Glenview, Illinois.
http://www.physicsclassroom.com/about.cfm

Index

Page numbers in **bold** refer to full articles; page numbers in *italic* refer to illustrations and captions.